ome into our Southern Kitchen and make yourself happy with some good Old-Fashioned Southern Cooking. Here you will discover some big puffy Dumplings in the Chicken Stew on the kitchen range, a serving bowl of Red Flannel Hash from the hill country, and a pot full of Turnips with Cheese. You could help yourself to a salad plate of Home Grown Tomatoes and Cucumbers with tasty Homemade Mayonnaise, and don't forget the Pecan Mini Pies.

Chicken & Dumplings

1   hen, remove skin and fat
1   cup milk
3   Tbsp. flour
    Thyme
    Bay leaves
    Dumplings (recipe follows)

If you want a really old-fashioned chicken stew, buy a hen. Cut it up and remove the skin and fat. Put it in a pot with enough water to barely cover it. You will cook it for 3 to 4 hours. After 1 hour, add 1 cup of milk and 3 Tbsp. of flour. Stir the flour in with some thyme and a couple of bay leaves. Add water to it whenever necessary. Near the end of 3 hours, make some dumplings and begin to reduce the gravy so that it thickens well, but enough to drop the dumplings in.

Dumplings

2   cups flour
2   tsp. baking powder
½   tsp. salt
2   Tbsp. butter flavored shortening
2   egg yolks
½   cup cold milk

Sift together flour, baking powder, and salt. Cut in butter flavored shortening with a pastry cutter. Mix and cut until all of it is of the same texture. Mix egg yolks and cold milk, beat well. Quickly mix this into the flour mixture until coarsely mixed. Drop by Tbsp. into the hot chicken gravy. Cook until they are puffed up and thoroughly done. You will want to turn them over. May also want to remove one and cut into it to make sure it is done. (If you have leftovers, remove the dumplings and save them in a separate container, or they will soak up the gravy and get soggy).

When the evenings get chilly, just fix a pot of hot Ground Beef Chili. The Mixed Bean Salad takes care of the beans that aren't in the Chili. Melt Sharp Cheddar Cheese on thick slices of Toasted Sour Dough Bread and finish the evening with a wedge of old timey Rhubarb Pie, with it's bright pink color peeking through the lattice top. Our family always considered this a Sunday night supper.

Rhubarb Pie

Cut up enough rhubarb to fill a 9" pie pan.

3 Tbsp. flour
1 cup sugar
1 egg, beaten
1 recipe plain pastry or use prepared folded pie crust
Nutmeg, if you like it

Sift flour and sugar together, beat in the egg, and add the rhubarb. Stir carefully. Unfold one round of the thawed pie crust and lay it carefully in the pan. Push out from the center a little and into the edge of the pan. Leave a little overhang. The red rhubarb makes a pretty pie, so it is nice to use a lattice top, but it is not essential. Cut the other round of pie crust into thin strips. If they break in the handling, just moisten and push them together again. You can put half of the strips one way, and the other half crosswise, but if you have time, it is nice to weave them in and out. When you need to go underneath a strip, just raise it or gently lay it back on itself, weave the cross strip underneath, and put the first back in place. Sounds complicated, but it becomes very easy to do with a little practice. Dampen the rim as you attach the strips, and then crimp the edges of the pie crust with your finger tips, or run a crimping tool around it.

Tomatoes, Cucumbers & Homemade Mayonnaise

MAYONNAISE:

2   eggs
½   tsp. salt
¼   tsp. red pepper
½   tsp. dry mustard
½   tsp. sugar
3   Tbsp. lemon juice
2   cups olive/peanut oil
1   Tbsp. boiling water

Break the eggs and put them into a blender. Add all the seasonings and only 1 Tbsp. lemon juice. Add the oil, drop by drop, beating continually, until about ⅓ of it is used up. Add the other 2 Tbsp. of lemon juice, and keep beating, then the remainder of the oil in a thin stream, while still beating. Add 1 Tbsp. boiling water, when the oil is all used up. Serve over fresh sliced tomatoes, and cucumbers.

Hill Country Red Flannel Hash

This is a traditional dish for using up leftover corned beef or roast beef and boiled potatoes. Start by cutting up about 6 or 8 potatoes and shredding or chopping 2 cups of meat. Chop up a large onion, a little bacon or salt pork, then fry together. Add the shredded meat, the cut potatoes, and some cut up fresh cooked or drained canned beets - about 2 cups. Season well with salt and pepper, mix thoroughly, and add enough beef broth to make it nicely moist. You can also add a little of the beet juice, if you want it redder. Ladle it into a good sized baking dish, and bake it at 350 degrees until crusty. This is a very tasty, colorful dish, and comes to us out of the Southern Hill Country.

Melted Cheddar on Thick Toast

Cut thick slices of sourdough bread. Toast well on one side. Toast the other side lightly, remove from toaster or broiler, place a thick slab of sharp Cheddar cheese on top of each, and put back in until cheese melts. Do this just when you are ready to serve. It is a great accompaniment to Chili.

Ground Beef Chili

1   Lb. ground beef
1   large onion, chopped
1   clove garlic, crushed
2   Tbsp. chili powder
1   can beef stock
1   can tomatoes
1   tsp. cumin
1   tsp. oregano
     Salt & pepper to taste

Brown ground meat in a large skillet. Add onion and garlic while it is cooking, stir often until everything is well cooked. Transfer ingredients to a large stew pot. Run tomatoes through a food processor until there are no lumps in the sauce. Add seasonings, beef stock and the tomatoes. Let the chili sauce simmer slowly until all the flavors have blended. Please your own taste. Add a little water if necessary, and add more beef stock or tomatoes if you wish. To thicken it slightly, sprinkle in a little flour and stir well, while it is cooking. Some of you will want more chili powder or hot sauce. This recipe does not call for beans, but if you add beans to it, serve it with a different salad than the Mixed Bean Salad. It will be too much for the palate.

Mixed Bean Salad

1   can kidney beans
1   can cut green beans
1   can cut wax beans
1   small jar pimento bits
½   onion, sliced thinly
1   stalk celery, chopped fine
½   cup virgin olive oil
½   cup rice vinegar
3   Tbsp. sugar
½   tsp. garlic salt
2   tsp. paprika
     Salt & pepper to taste

Drain the beans and pimento bits. Mix together in a large bowl. Add onion, celery, olive oil, vinegar, and all the seasonings, stir well. Cover the bowl and let marinate overnight in the refrigerator.

*L*et the family help themselves in the kitchen to a Cream of Cabbage Soup that is rich with other tasty veggies and herbs. This is a meal that will stick to your ribs, because there are freshly made Drop Biscuits on the counter, and a bowl of Hot German Potato Salad. Many Germans settled in parts of Louisiana and Mississippi. They also knew how to make a Deep Dish Apple Pie.

Drop Biscuits

2 cups flour
4 tsp. baking powder
2 Tbsp. butter
1¼ cups milk
1 tsp. salt

Sift together all the dry ingredients. Work in shortening with finger tips or a pastry mixer. Add liquid gradually, stirring loosely to make a soft mixture, but don't overdo it. Drop by spoonfuls on a greased cookie sheet. Bake 12 to 15 minutes in a preheated 450 degree oven.

Cream of Cabbage Soup

2　Tbsp. butter
2　Tbsp. flour
2　cups milk
2　cups chicken broth
2　cups shredded cabbage
2　cups cubed potatoes
1　cup julienne carrots
1　cup slivered onions
1　tsp. dill
2　bay leaves

Melt butter, cream flour into it, and gradually add milk, then chicken stock. Slice cabbage and onions into very thin shreds. Add to the soup along with the potatoes and carrots. Season with finely chopped dill, the bay leaves, salt, and pepper to taste. Simmer until all of the ingredients are tender.

Cheese-Turnip Casserole

1½　Lbs. turnips, pared and sliced (end product about 4 cups)
3　Tbsp. butter
¼　cup chopped onion
¼　cup chopped green pepper
¼　cup finely chopped celery
1　cup milk/cream (or more)
½　cup grated Cheddar cheese
　　Snipped parsley
　　Paprika
　　Salt to taste
　　Seasoned bread crumbs

Cook turnips in enough water to cover, salted and boiling, until tender. Drain. Melt butter and fry vegetables until soft and translucent. Blend flour in slowly, smoothing it in with the butter as you add it. Add milk as you need it, to the desired consistency. Add cheese, salt, and pepper. Cook on low heat until melted into the sauce. Combine cheese sauce and turnips and pour into a baking dish or casserole of one quart capacity. Top with seasoned bread crumbs (optional). Dust top with paprika and sprinkle with parsley bits. Bake at 350 degrees until hot and bubbly.

Spicy German Potato Salad

2　Tbsp. olive oil
4　slices bacon, cut up
4　Irish potatoes
½　cup chopped onions
¼　cup chopped celery
¼　cup chopped parsley
2　Tbsp. balsamic vinegar
2　Tbsp. brown sugar
¼　cup sweet pickle relish
　　Salt & red pepper to taste

Slice potatoes thinly. Heat olive oil in a large deep skillet. Add bacon pieces and cook until brown, adding onions and celery when part way through. Drain off excess fat, but leave a little for flavor. Add potatoes and other ingredients and cook until potatoes are done. Stir gently while simmering until everything is hot and blended, but do not break up the potato slices.

Deep Dish Apple Pie

Use your favorite pie crust recipe or a frozen pie crust, because you are going to make a lattice topped pie in a deep dish. You will not use a bottom crust in this pie. Use a large and deep oven proof dish. Place a strip of crust around the inner side of the dish, but not over the bottom. Fill with the apple mixture. Then cut strips for the lattice top. If you have a crinkle edged cutter wheel, it will make them pretty, but it is not necessary. Dampen the strip of pie dough you put around the edge, so the ends of the strips will stick to it. It is nice to weave the strips one at a time, but you can put on one layer going all the same way, and then cross it with the other half of the strips. If you break a strip, just dampen the broken ends and stick them together. When you have finished, trim the ends that hang over, dampen the edge by dipping your fingers in water, and put another strip on top. Then crimp the edges together.

FILLING:

8　Granny Smith Apples
¾　cup sugar
¼　tsp. nutmeg
¼　cup cinnamon
¼　tsp. salt
½　Tbsp. butter
2　tsp. lemon juice
　　Grated lemon zest

Pare and core apples, cut each in 8 wedges. Place them around the plate, and add toward the center, placing them in rings. Put another layer on top of the first. Mix all of the remaining ingredients and sprinkle over the apples, but save the butter to dot over the top. Set the pie in the bottom of a preheated 450 degree oven for 10 minutes. Then cut the heat down to 350 degrees and change the pie to the middle shelf. Bake 35 to 40 more minutes until nicely browned. If the edge gets too brown, put on pie guards or a strip of aluminum foil. This can be done before you start to bake the pie.

*P*erhaps you aren't as hungry some evenings, so have a bowl of French Onion Soup with toast rounds floating on the top, each topped with a sprinkle of grated cheese, as our French ancestors would have done. The Chicken Salad made with Apples and Walnuts is hearty enough to hold you until morning. The Black Bottom Pie has a surprise for you, underneath the Creamy Custard top.

French Onion Soup

3 Tbsp. butter
6 sweet onions
6 cups beef broth
   Dash of Worcestershire sauce
   Salt & black pepper to taste
   Romano cheese, grated
   Marsala/Sherry wine (optional)
   French bread or French rolls

Melt butter in a large heavy pot. Slice onions very thinly and stir them in the butter until soft and golden. Add beef broth and seasonings and simmer until very hot. Slice thin rounds of French bread or French rolls, and toast until dry and hard. When serving the soup, float a few rounds on the surface of each bowl of soup and sprinkle with Romano cheese. Serve an assortment of crispy crackers and buttered toast rounds or triangles with the soup and salad.

Rich Potato Salad

10 medium potatoes
6   hard boiled eggs
6   green onions, chopped
3   ribs celery, chopped fine
1   bell pepper, diced small
1   small jar pimento bits
½   cup sweet pickle relish
    Salt & pepper to taste
½   cup mayonnaise
1   Tbsp. lemon juice
1   Tbsp. sugar
1   Tbsp. dark mustard
½   pint whipping cream

Peel (or not, as you prefer) and cook potatoes. Peel and dice eggs. If you want a yellow salad, remove yolks, mash and mix with mayonnaise later. Add all chopped vegetables and sweet pickles. As you mix these together, add the proper amount of salt and pepper, check for taste. Now add yolks, vinegar, sugar and mustard to the mayonnaise and mix thoroughly with the potatoes. Let stand in the refrigerator until cool. Now add ½ pint of whipping cream. This will make a wonderfully rich and creamy salad. Never put this salad in a deep bowl to chill, as it will not cool through to the center. It must be well chilled to be safe.

Chicken Salad with Apple & Walnuts

2 cups diced chicken meat
1 cup walnuts, broken pieces
   (reserve some for garnish)
2 cups apples, peeled, diced
   Torn pieces of leaf lettuce
   Dash of salt
   Lemon juice

Mix chicken and walnut pieces together. Add diced apples which have been sprinkled with lemon/orange juice to keep fresh. Salt lightly. Place on a bed of lettuce on a large platter, or individual salad plates. Serve with lemon cream dressing.

LEMON CREAM DRESSING:

Stir 1 can of pineapple juice into 1 cup of mayonnaise until it is smooth. Add lemon juice until you get the desired degree of acidity. Serve in a bowl and let guests serve themselves. You may garnish with grapes or pineapple chunks.

Black Bottom Pie

1 unbaked pie shell or 1 chocolate crumb crust. Beat 4 egg yolks. Slowly add 2 cups scalded milk, stirring all the while. Then mix ½ cup sugar with 1 Tbsp. cornstarch and stir into the egg mixture. Cook in a double boiler until it will leave a coating on the spoon. Add 1 tsp. of vanilla.

FIRST LAYER:

Take out 1 cup of the custard and add 6 oz. of semisweet chocolate chips. Stir until chips are melted. Pour into shell and chill.

SECOND LAYER:

Start this layer when the hot custard has cooled and thickened somewhat. Soften 1 Tbsp. Knox gelatin in ¼ cup cold water. Add the rest of the warm custard. Stir until gelatin is dissolved and cool. Beat egg whites until foamy, add ¼ tsp. cream of tarter, and continue beating at high speed, gradually adding ½ cup of sugar. Continue beating until the whites stand in stiff peaks. Fold the cooled custard gelatin mixture and the beaten egg whites together. Pour over the chocolate layer and chill.

*M*ost Southern Homes always have a warm welcome waiting for you, even if they don't have a sign out. If you drop in on a day when they have cooked a good Southern Fish Chowder, I feel sure they will invite you to have a bowl full, with a piece of Hot Cornbread on the side. The Dressed Up Tomatoes can be fixed in a jiffy, and easy to make Egg Custard is sure to comfort your tummy.

Dressed up Tomatoes

This is one cooking trick that works very well in a microwave. Cut large tomatoes in half, horizontally. Turn the halves with the cut side up. Place on a tray in the microwave on full power for 2 or 3 minutes. Remove and mash lightly with a fork. Sprinkle with a little salt, pepper and some seasoned bread crumbs, and mash that layer in a little. Top with a sprinkle of Romano cheese and a pat of butter, then return to the oven for 2 or 3 more minutes until all is well melted. Remove and serve. Sprinkle a little paprika on top and garnish with parsley.

Egg Custard

3 eggs
3 cups milk
1 tsp. vanilla
1 cup sugar
¼ tsp. salt

Scald milk until tiny bubbles form around the edges, but do not boil. Beat eggs lightly, stir in sugar and salt. Add scalded milk, a little at a time to the egg mixture until you have a warm, well stirred mixture. Then add the rest of the milk. Stir again and pour into 6 buttered custard cups, but leave some room at the top. Place the cups in a pan of hot water, dust with nutmeg and bake in a 350 degree oven until firm. Insert the point of a knife to test. It should come out clean, if the custard is well set.

Oyster Stew in Patty Shells

Cook 1 small onion, chopped very fine, in 2 Tbsp. oil until soft and yellow. Add 2 Tbsp. of flour and brown well, but not too dark. Add a little water gradually until there is enough brown gravy to cook the oysters in it. Add a dash of Worcestershire sauce, ½ tsp. tarragon, salt, and pepper to taste. When sauce is the right color and consistency, (not too thick and not too thin) add the oysters and cook until the edges curl. Add more water if necessary, a little at a time. The patty shells should be browned and hot when the oyster stew is added. Allow about 4 oysters for each shell. Remove the lid of each patty shell, spoon the oysters into the shells, place the little lid back on top, and serve immediately, as a first course that will whet the appetites of your guests.

Vinaigrette Sauce:

Mix ⅓ cup each of virgin olive oil and rice vinegar, 1 Tbsp. lemon juice, 2 Tbsp. sugar, ¼ tsp. dry mustard, ¼ cup sweet pickle relish with a little of the juice, salt, and pepper to taste.

Hot Corn Bread Squares

1 cup yellow cornmeal
1½ cups milk
1 tsp. salt
2 Tbsp. butter
2½ tsp. baking powder
1 egg, separated

Simmer milk until tiny bubbles form around the edge, but do not boil. Add cornmeal and stir in salt and butter. Beat egg yolk and baking powder, add to mixture, stir really well. Grease an 8" x 8" square pan and heat in oven. Remove and immediately pour batter into the hot pan. This makes a good crust. Bake in a preheated 400 degree oven for 20 minutes. Serve hot, cut in squares.

Southern Fish & Potato Chowder

2 cups milk
1 cup chicken stock
1 cup half and half cream
2 Tbsp. flour
2 Tbsp. butter
2 cups cubed firm fish
½ tsp. thyme
1 yellow bell pepper, diced
1 sweet onion, diced
3 potatoes, boiled and cubed
2 cups corn kernels, plus milk scraped from cob
½ cup chopped parsley
Salt & pepper

Stir the flour well into 1 cup of the milk, then put all of the liquid, with the flour and fat, into a large stock pot and heat until bubbles form around the edge. Add all ingredients except parsley, salt, and pepper. Simmer until mixture is slightly thickened and add parsley and seasonings. Serve with a garnish of parsley and crisp saltine crackers.

Mixed Greens with Romano Cheese Salad

Tear pieces of iceberg lettuce, leaf lettuce, and spinach or any other lettuce you like. A mixture of different lettuces improves the flavor of the salad immeasurably. Toss with the vinaigrette sauce and sprinkle with Romano Cheese. (Romano is not as strong as Parmesan)

Fresh Flounder is always available in Mississippi and Louisiana, because of their proximity to the Gulf of Mexico. It is lovely baked and served on a bed of Creamed Spinach. But first, try an appetizer of Oysters in a delicious Brown Gravy served in hot, crisp Patty Shells. Southern cooks have been making Mustard Sauce for years, but try stirring boiled potatoes into it. Delicious! Have a quick to fix Green Salad and for dessert one of the South's great Coconut Cream Pies.

Baked Flounder on Creamed Spinach

Clean, rinse lightly and wipe dry 2 large flounder fillets. Sprinkle an adequate amount of salt, pepper, and some ground rosemary or tarragon on both sides of the fillets and carefully rub it in. Melt ¼ cup of butter in a baking pan and brush some of it over the seasonings. Add a little lemon juice and white wine to the pan. Put the pan under the oven broiler to be sure it is at the broiling temperature before you put the fish in it. Now carefully lay the fish in the butter sauce. Place the pan back under the broiler and broil at your regular oven broiling temperature until nicely browned. Baste with the butter sauce at regular intervals. It is preferable not to turn the fish over and risk breaking it up. Check for doneness before it gets too dry, by using a fork, and seeing if the flesh is white, flaky and done to the bottom. It should be nice and crusty on the top. Remove the fish carefully with a large spatula and lay it on the bed of creamed spinach. Garnish with lemon wedges.

Creamed Spinach

Cook well washed, trimmed, and chopped spinach for 15 minutes, or follow the directions on 2 packs of frozen spinach. Drain well and fold it into a cream sauce. Season it with salt and pepper, a little nutmeg, and a dash of lemon juice. Place it in an oval platter, ready for the fish to be placed in the center of it.

Potatoes in Mustard Sauce

Cut cooled boiled potatoes in pieces, not too large. Make a white sauce, or use canned Creamy Onion Soup, add sprinkles of tarragon and parsley, and ½ tsp. of dry mustard. Stir in ¼ stick butter or margarine, and heat well. Serve with sprinkles of bacon bits (real or imitation) over the top, and a dash of paprika.

Coconut Cream Pie

2	cups milk
½	cup flour
¼	cup sugar
⅛	tsp. salt
2	eggs, beaten
2	Tbsp. butter
1	tsp. almond extract
	Whipped cream
2	cups fresh shredded or canned angel flake coconut

Use a baked or graham cracker pie crust. Heat 1 cup milk over low heat in a sauce pan until tiny bubbles appear around the edge, but do not boil. In a bowl, mix the salt and flour into the sugar, and stir in the other cup of milk. Then add the whole mixture to the hot milk and stir well. Cook for another 15 minutes over low heat, until mixture thickens. (A double boiler may be used if you worry about scorching the milk). Add the hot mixture a little at a time, to the beaten egg yolks. When part of it is well blended, pour it all back into the hot milk in the pan. Cook another 3 minutes. Add the shredded coconut to the cream mixture, but save enough out for the topping. Cool and add almond extract. Pour this concoction into the pie shell. Chill until set. Cover with whipped cream or Cool Whip, lightly toast the remainder of the shredded coconut, and sprinkle over the top.

A Catfish Supper sounds sort of back woodsy, but this fish is highly prized in the South. We now have many catfish farms in Mississippi and Louisiana. It is light and tasty. Serve it with colorful Tomato Rice and Sweet and Sour Beets. Fruit Filled Dumplings are so easy to fix, if you buy your Puff Paste, and they will make your guests so happy.

Simmered Catfish

Season both sides of catfish fillets with tarragon, salt, and red or black pepper. Gently pat seasonings into the fillets with your fingers and dust lightly with flour. Peel a tomato, push out all of the seeds and juice, and cut the outside into thin strips. Finely chop half of a medium onion. Melt 2 Tbsp. butter in a skillet. Carefully lay the fillets in the hot fat. Add the onions and tomato bits around them. This does not make a heavy tomato sauce. When fillets are nicely browned on one side, turn them over and brown the other side. Serve with a small amount of the butter, tomato and onion sauce poured over the fish.

Sweet & Sour Beets

Open 2 cans of sliced or julienne beets. Drain and save juice. Melt 2 Tbsp. of butter, gradually cream in 2 Tbsp. of flour, and add the beet juice little by little until you get the consistency you want. If it is not red enough to suit you, add a drop of red food coloring. It should look like red velvet. Add ¼ cup lemon juice (depending upon your taste), 1 tsp. sugar, salt, and cayenne pepper to taste. Blend well and stir in beets, letting the whole mixture simmer until hot and bubbly. Add a little water if it gets too thick.

Tossed Greens with Croutons

Tear green leaf lettuce, small young spinach, and iceberg lettuce into small pieces. Add bits of red and white kale for color and added flavor. Toss with a vinaigrette dressing and sprinkle with croutons.

Vinaigrette Dressing

Mix ½ cup rice or cane vinegar with ½ cup olive oil and ½ cup white wine. Add 1 Tbsp. sugar (or more to taste), a little chopped tarragon or basil (fresh if possible), and 2 Tbsp. sweet pickle relish. Season with ½ tsp. each of dry mustard and paprika. Add salt and pepper to taste. Shake well before using.

Tomato Rice

Cook 1 ½ cups rice in 3 quarts of lightly salted boiling water for 18 minutes and drain in a colander. Fry a chopped pepper, chopped onion, and a couple of ribs of finely chopped celery until tender. Add 1 small can of mushrooms and 1 can of stewed tomatoes, chopped up. Add 1 Tbsp. of Worcestershire sauce, a dash of vinegar, and 1 tsp. of sugar. Sprinkle in garlic salt to taste, and cook until it is well blended. Remove from stove and stir in hot rice.

Fruit Filled Dumplings

Buy Puff Paste from the freezer section of your store. Cut into 4" squares. Peel and core the apples, peaches or other fruit. Place one on each square of puff paste. (You can cut the peach in half to take out the pit and then put the halves back together again in the puff paste.) Mix cinnamon and nutmeg with some sugar and fill the core of the peach with some of it. Sprinkle grated cheese on top and dot with butter. Fold one corner up over the top. Moisten the pastry with water and press together pretty well as you do this. Make holes in the puff paste here and there, and bake in a preheated 350 degree oven for 30 minutes, or until it is a nice golden brown.

irlitons, baked with small Shrimp and elegantly served in a lovely room, make the most delectable dish you can imagine. Don't kill the delicate flavor with strongly flavored large shrimp, too much seasoning, or any side dishes that are too robust. The creamy Berry Parfait will impress your guests and pamper their palate.

Baked Mirlitons & Shrimp

4   vegetable pears
4   green onions
1   stick butter
1   Lb. small shrimp (cleaned)
2   bay leaves
1   Tbsp. chopped parsley
1   cup seasoned bread crumbs
    Salt & pepper to taste
    Paprika

These vegetable pears are called mirlitons in the French South and chayotes in the Southwest and in Mexico. Both the pears and the baby shrimp have a very delicate flavor, so we don't want to spoil it with a lot of heavy seasoning. Cut the pears in half and boil until tender. Scoop out the pulp and chop it well until there are no lumps, but don't put it through a food processor. It will turn into soup. Chop the green onions finely, including part of the tender green tops. Simmer onions in butter until soft, add pear pulp and bay leaves. Continue cooking until everything is totally cooked. Add parsley and shrimp and cook until shrimp turns pink. Remove bay leaves and season to taste. Add part of the bread crumbs, but save enough to use on the top. Put in a baking dish, top with bread crumbs, drizzle melted butter over the top, and dust with paprika. Bake at 350 degrees for 20 to 30 minutes, until the top looks crusty.

Leeks & Potatoes Au Gratin

2   cups cooked potatoes, cut in
    rather small chunks
10 leeks, washed well and cut in
    one inch pieces
½   cup grated Monterey Jack
    cheese
    Half and half cream
¼   cup margarine or butter
1   clove garlic, crushed
    Salt & pepper to taste

Melt the butter in a large frying pan, and add the leeks. Stir over low heat until almost tender. Add the cooked potato pieces, the crushed garlic, and a little of the cream. As the mixture cooks, stir in the garlic, salt and pepper and more cream as necessary. When it is nearly done, stir in the cheese. Serve in a large platter or bowl.

Berry, Cream, & Tapioca Parfait

Use 2 cans or 2 frozen pkgs. of raspberries and drain. Use tall slender stem goblets. Make up a quantity of Tapioca pudding, according to directions on the pkg. Use 1 small carton of Cool Whip, La Creme, or chocolate Cool Whip. Put a layer of pudding in the bottom of the glass, then add a layer of berries, and on top of that, spoon in a layer of cream. Repeat. Chill well before serving.

Green Pea & Ham Soup

½   cup dried split peas
1   qt. cold water
1   small onion, chopped
1   cup milk
3   Tbsp. butter
1   Tbsp. flour
½   tsp. salt
    Pepper to taste
2   cups seasoning ham, chopped
    into bits

Pick over peas and soak overnight. Drain, add cold water, and cook over medium heat. In a separate pot, fry onions in 1 Tbsp. of butter until soft. Add the onions and ham to the soup. Heat remainder of butter, flour, salt, and pepper, and cook together in the pot the onions were in. Add milk gradually until all is well blended and creamy. Stir into the pot of soup. Add more milk whenever needed. When the soup is served, sprinkle a few croutons on the top.

Boiled Okra in Oil & Vinegar

Cook fresh baby okra in boiling water until tender. Chill and serve as a salad with oil and vinegar. (Some people prefer it hot).

almon is not a native fish in our part of the country, but Salmon Croquettes are an old favorite. It is nice to serve them with a White Sauce. An Avocado-Grapefruit Salad accompanies them quite well. In the early summer, the natives grow restless, because they are waiting for the Pole Beans to mature, and the Baby New Potatoes to appear in the market. They have to be cooked together, of course, and flavored with ham from the smoke house. Angel Pie presents a luscious dessert.

Salmon Croquettes with White Sauce

Pick over canned salmon, (remove all the dark parts and bones), until you have 2 cups of flaked salmon (or use leftover cooked salmon). Chop 1 small onion and fry in 1 tsp. of butter until soft. Stir in 2 Tbsp. flour and some finely chopped parsley, chives, and tarragon. Cook until the mixture is a smooth paste. Add a little milk if necessary, but keep it thick. Remove from fire and beat in 2 eggs, and slowly add hot mixture to the eggs in a large bowl, stirring all the while. Season with a little salt and a little red pepper. Stir the salmon into the milk and egg mixture and then add seasoned bread crumbs, a few at a time until the mixture is thick enough to form into small pear shaped mounds. Chill, roll fish mounds in egg batter, and then in bread crumbs. Fry in deep fat or bake in oven until golden brown. Garnish with sprigs of parsley and lemon wedges. Serve with a White Sauce. (See page 23).

Fruit Filled Angel Pie

4   egg whites
¼   tsp. cream of tartar
1   cup fine granulated sugar
1   tsp. almond extract

Beat egg whites until foamy. Add ¼ tsp. cream of tartar and beat again. Gradually add the cup of sugar, and finally the almond extract. This mixture should be beaten until it stands in stiff peaks. Spread this meringue gently into a buttered 9" pyrex or oven proof pie plate. Let the edges stand higher and leave a sort of hollow in the center. Bake in a 275 degree oven for 40 minutes.

APRICOT FILLING:

Soak apricots in boiling water until soft. Drain and measure out 1 cup of the pulp, beat in enough sugar to sweeten to your taste. Fold this into 1 cup of whipped cream or Cool Whip and spoon into center of pie.

STRAWBERRY FILLING:

Crush a small carton of ripe strawberries, and sweeten to taste. Fold into whipped cream.

ORANGE OR LEMON FILLING:

Beat 4 egg yolks until thick with 4 Tbsp. of sugar and 4 Tbsp. of one of the juices. Simmer over hot water. When the mixture has thickened enough, and is not too liquid, cool it and then spoon it into the meringue pie. You may also add dollops of whipped cream or Cool Whip over the top of the pie when you serve it.

Pole Beans, Ham & New Potatoes

1   Lb. green pole beans
2   dozen small new potatoes
    Pieces of ham, leave some fat
1   large sweet onion, chopped
2   Tbsp. butter
2   Tbsp. Worcestershire sauce
2   Tbsp. Balsamic vinegar
    Salt and black pepper to taste

Trim beans and cut in pieces. Wash potatoes and drop in boiling water with skins on. Cook 10 minutes. Add beans and salt. Cook 5 minutes more, or until all are tender. Fry ham in butter and add onions. When onions are golden, add beans, potatoes, and some of the bean water. Add seasonings and cook together long enough to be cooked down and well flavored. Add more water if necessary.

Avocado & Grapefruit Salad

Quarter avocado, and remove the rind carefully. Cut longwise into fairly thin slices. Sprinkle with lemon or lime juice to keep from turning dark. Cut fresh grapefruit sections, or buy a refrigerator jar of them. Place on salad plates, on green leafy lettuce, in a pinwheel design. Alternate avocado and grapefruit pieces. Serve with poppy seed or French dressing.

Southern Fried Chicken is about as far South as you can get, in the world of good food. A really rich Potato Salad with real whipping cream, and Stuffed Eggs, are traditionally served with it, and the Bunches of Grapes Salads, served on grape bordered plates, add a perky new note to the meal. Everything, including the Crunchy Topped Cake, tastes better out by the little cabin.

Batter Fried Chicken

2 young chickens
1 egg
½ cup milk
   Flour
   Salt and pepper

Cut each chicken in 4 pieces. Beat egg in milk. Put some flour in a brown bag and season with salt and pepper. Dip chicken pieces in egg mixture and shake each piece in the bag with seasoned flour. Fry in deep fat on medium heat. Remove each piece as it is done.

Bunches of Grapes Salad

Cut firm pears in half. Hard pears can be stewed in a little water till tender. Core carefully. Turn flat side down. Frost pear halves with cream cheese. Cut green or red grapes in half and cover pears with halves, sticking them to the cream cheese. (Small grapes fit better than larger ones). Garnish with chicory, water cress, or flat leaved parsley at the stem end of the pears.

Stuffed Eggs

Take eggs out of refrigerator and bring to room temperature. Puncture large end of each egg with an egg pricker. Place in pot, cover with water, and gradually bring to a boil. Turn the heat down to a good simmer. Don't let the eggs bounce around in rapidly boiling water. Salt the water. Cook for 35 minutes. Remove from heat, carefully pour off the hot water, and put the pot under a faucet. Let cold water run into the pot and overflow until they are totally cooled. Do not hit the shell hard to break it, or you may damage the white underneath. Crush it gently, all around, with your fingers, and then peel it. Cut the egg in half. Set the white halves on an egg plate, and gently remove the yolks and put them in a bowl. Mash the yolks, add mayonnaise, wet or dry mustard, salt, cayenne pepper, lemon juice, sweet pickle relish, and chopped pimento. Stuff the eggs. You will be better satisfied if you taste the mixture as you go, and learn the amount of each ingredient that pleases you.

Crunchy Topped Quick Cake

1⅓ cup biscuit mix
¾ cup sugar
3 Tbsp. butter
1 egg
¾ cup milk
1 tsp. pure vanilla

Heat oven to 325 degrees. Grease and flour an oblong pyrex dish. Mix sugar and biscuit mix. Add softened butter, egg, and ¼ cup of the milk. Beat with a hand mixer for 1 minute. Add remainder of milk and vanilla. Beat ½ minute. Pour into pan and bake 25 to 35 minutes or until it browns and starts to shrink from the pan. Cover with topping.

TOPPING:

Mix 3 Tbsp. of butter, softened, with ⅓ cup brown sugar, 2 Tbsp. half and half or cream, and ¾ cup chopped pecans. Spread on baked cake. Place 3" under broiler (on low heat) until mixture bubbles (3 to 5 minutes) DO NOT BURN! Store in refrigerator. When you cut a piece, zap it about 30 seconds in the microwave and it will taste as if it had just been baked.

In the South, people of any and all colors ate Soul Food, and where better to consume it, than the handy kitchen table, close to the source of supply? When Greens are Cooked with Pickled Pork, a liquor of great taste is created, and the name "Pot Likker" has a magic sound. It conjures up memories of breaking up crusty Cornbread into such a liquid. Our menu is completed with a Creamed Corn Casserole, Gingerbread with Apple Sauce, and tall mugs of cold buttermilk.

Creamed Corn Casserole

2   Tbsp. butter, melted
2   Tbsp. flour
2   cups milk
1   tsp. salt
½   tsp. dry mustard
2   cups corn and corn "milk"
2   eggs
    Dash of Worcestershire sauce
½   cup chopped green onions
    Seasoned bread crumbs

Mix melted butter, flour, milk and seasonings. Beat eggs lightly, mix with corn, and add the combination to the whole mixture. Add the Worcestershire sauce and green onions; stir well. Pour into a casserole that is big enough to keep the recipe from bubbling over the top. Top with bread crumbs and pats of butter. Bake in a 350 degree oven for 25 minutes, or until top is crusty and bubbly.

Greens, "Pot Likker" & Pickle Meat

Wash and tear into large pieces a mixture of greens. Throw away any large midribs of the leaves. Use any combination of greens you like, such as turnip, mustard, and spinach. Other possibilities are beet leaves, chard or kale. Cut up 1 Lb. or more of pickled pork, salt meat, or ham, and best of all, put a hambone in. You can also peel and use turnip bottoms, dice them and add them to the cooking about half way through. Start with some fat or oil at the bottom of a large stew pot. Fry the greens, turning them and not letting them stay on the bottom long enough to burn. As soon as all are wilted, add enough water for the greens to cook in, and add more later if necessary. Season with salt, Tabasco, Worcestershire sauce, and you may even add some beef stock to give the dish more flavor. Cook a long time, until everything is tender and well cooked down. Serve in large bowls with plenty of "pot likker" and cornbread, because everyone has to dunk the chunks of cornbread into the liquor.

Spicy Hot Cornbread

2   cups scalded milk
2   cups yellow cornmeal
1   tsp. salt
2   Tbsp. oil
2½   tsp. baking powder
2   eggs, beaten
1   tsp. cayenne pepper
8   slices of bacon

Mix milk and cornmeal, and stir in baking powder, eggs, pepper and bacon, cut into 1" pieces. Pour the oil into the pan that is to be used for the cornbread and heat until it is red hot, but don't let it catch on fire. Immediately drain the hot oil from the pan into the cornbread mixture, which will bubble and spew, but this improves the taste and the crust. Stir the mix quickly and immediately pour the batter into the hot pan. Bake at 400 degrees for 30 minutes, until golden brown.

** *If you like your cornbread sweet as well as spicy, add a little sugar to the recipe. If you want the cornbread to be really hot, you may add some sliced Jalapeño peppers.*

Gingerbread & AppleSauce

2   cups sifted cake flour
2   tsp. baking powder
¼   tsp. baking soda
2   tsp. ginger
½   tsp. salt
⅓   cup butter flavored shortening
½   cup sugar
1   egg, beaten
⅔   cup molasses
¾   cup buttermilk

Sift all dry ingredients together. Beat the sugar into the shortening until light and frothy. Beat the egg and molasses into it. Now add a little of the dry ingredients to the mix and then a little of the buttermilk. Continue adding these two things alternately until they are all used up. Pour the batter into a greased square pan. Bake in a 350 degree oven for 45 minutes or until a toothpick comes out clean. Cut in squares and serve hot or cold, with applesauce on it, topped with a dollop of whipped cream.

oast Chicken is traditionally a Sunday Dinner dish. Favored accompaniments are Baked Potatoes, topped with all the trimmings, English Peas in a White Sauce, and colorful salad with yellow and red peppers. The best Sunday dessert of all has to be Strawberry Shortcake, made with the good old Southern Sweet Biscuit Dough.

Roast Chicken

Wash bird before working with it. Wipe dry and rub inside and out with butter/margarine, and then rub with salt and pepper. Place in a roasting pan, breast side down. Legs can be tied together and wings folded behind the back. Allow 25 minutes per pound for a 4-6 Lb. bird. Bake at 350 degrees. At about half the time period required, turn the breast side up and make a tent of aluminum foil to cover the breast. Bacon strips may be placed across the breast to protect it from drying out. Chicken should be tender and brown. Untie the legs, place bird on a warm platter, garnish with parsley, and serve hot and juicy.

Tossed Greens with Colored Pepper Bits

Use 2 or 3 kinds of lettuce, including the red radiccio, if you can find it, because it gives more flavor to the salad. Tear in bite sized pieces, and toss in a vinaigrette or other dressing. Cut red, yellow, and green bell peppers in bits and sprinkle over the top. The yellow peppers are so sweet they almost taste like pickles.

Baked Potatoes with Trimmings

Bake Irish potatoes until tender. Cut in half, and mash fairly well in the shell. Add a little butter, some salt, and pepper and mash a little more. Lightly mix in some sour cream and chopped green onion tops, with bacon bits on top. Serve while still hot.

White Sauce

In a skillet, melt 2 Tbsp. butter. Remove from heat and slowly cream in 2 Tbsp. flour, until it is like a smooth paste. Then gradually add hot milk, blending it thoroughly as you add, smoothing out any lumps. Depends on the thickness/thinness of the sauces you are wanting, will determine the amount of milk to be added, so judge accordingly. Salt lightly and cook until smooth and thick. If you do this carefully, it should take 15 or 20 minutes.

Creamed English Peas

Simmer fresh or frozen green peas until tender. Add the peas to the white sauce, and stir the whole mixture together gently, so the peas will not be broken up.

Sweet Biscuit Strawberry Shortcake

2   cups flour
1   Tbsp. sugar
3   tsp. baking powder
⅓   cup milk
½   tsp. salt
4   Tbsp. butter
1   egg, beat well
    Whipped cream
    Strawberries or other fruit

Mix and roll out as for biscuits, (see page 49). Cut 2 large squares and place one in a greased pan. Spread lightly with melted butter and place the other half on top of it. Bake 12 minutes in a preheated 450 degree oven. To serve, split with a fork and spread with butter. Spread partially crushed, sweetened strawberries between layers and on the top. Save a few whole ones to place over the whipped cream you will serve on it.

or a good while now, people in the South have been very big on Fried Turkey, and once you taste the meat of one, you will understand why. Twice Baked Yams have an extra flavor to match that of the turkey. Broccoli and Rice Casserole and Ambrosia complete the menu. Jezebel Sauce, which I always connect with Mississippi, is wonderful with all meats, hot or cold.

Deep Fried Turkey Roll

It is possible to fry a whole turkey, but this is best done for you at a restaurant or commercial kitchen, because it takes a huge pot. It is becoming a very popular thing to do, because it tastes great. The idea seems to have begun in the South. The easiest thing to do in your home, is to buy a boneless turkey, which is really a turkey roll, all trussed up and easy to handle. It will fit into a large "home size" pot. Heat some peanut oil, enough to get up a good heat. I can't say "enough to cover", because the turkey will eventually start to float. Rub the turkey well with a mixture of seasonings. (See list below.) Get the temperature up to 290 degrees. A 12 Lb. turkey will take 35 to 45 minutes, so judge accordingly. Probably add 4 to 5 minutes per pound. You CANNOT judge if the turkey is done just because it floats, in spite of what your friends may tell you. The turkey must reach an internal temperature of 165 degrees.

SEASONING MIX:

3 tsp. salt
6 tsp. ground basil
2 tsp. each of oregano, thyme and paprika
1 tsp. each of white pepper, black pepper, garlic powder and onion powder

The white pepper effects a different part of the mouth and gives the other seasonings a good "underlayment" of flavor. (If this is not enough seasoning for a large turkey, double the recipe) This recipe comes from Gene Rives, who also fried the turkey for this picture.

Broccoli & Rice Casserole

Any vegetable can be used in this casserole. Break broccoli or cauliflower, or both into florets, (or cut zucchini or yellow squash into chunks), and cook in salt water until barely tender. Fry 1 finely chopped onion in a stick of butter. Add 2 cups cooked rice to the onions and stir around in the butter. Add Worcestershire sauce to your taste, salt, pepper, and garlic salt and stir well. Add the vegetables, 1 can of creamy onion soup, and if necessary, a little milk. Heat and stir until well mixed and nicely moist. Pour into a baking dish. Top with seasoned bread crumbs and dot with butter if you wish, or just sprinkle with paprika and bake without a topping. Bake in 350 degree oven until bubbly hot.

Twice Baked Yams

Prick the skins of whole washed yams and bake 4 minutes in the microwave. Test with a fork. (If they are too hard to cut and mash, put back in the microwave for 1 or 2 minutes until tender). Remove and cut in half, lengthwise. Mash each half with a fork, all the way to the bottom, but do not tear the "boat" of skin that holds it. Put a pat of butter on each and mash it in. Then sprinkle with brown sugar and heat until butter and sugar begin to melt into the yam. If you want to bake them in a regular oven, it will take about 40 to 50 minutes. Nearing the end of that time, you can do the cutting and mashing, and add the butter and brown sugar.

Ambrosia

6 navel oranges
1 large can crushed pineapple
1 fresh coconut (save milk to drink)
1 bunch green grapes
1 large can pitted Bing cherries (or maraschino cherries)
1 cup miniature marshmallows
1 cup sour cream
½ cup powdered sugar

Grate coconut (or buy a can of angel flake coconut). Peel oranges. Separate out wedges (or use orange sections in refrigerated jar). The fresh orange sections taste better than the canned mandarin oranges. Mix all ingredients together. Let stand overnight in refrigerator. (Miniature marshmallows may be mixed in).

Jezebel Sauce

1 8 oz. jar pineapple preserves
1 8 oz. jar apple jelly
1 Tbsp. freshly ground black pepper
1½ tsp. dry mustard
3-4 Tbsp. prepared horseradish

Combine all ingredients, stir well, and refrigerate. Serve over a block of cream cheese as an appetizer, or serve with hot or cold meats. It is also a great sauce for baby carrots.

*I*n the "Country English" atmosphere often found in the South, tender juicy little Broiled Lamb Chops are well loved, and of course, they must be accompanied by Mint Jelly. Browned Potato Chunks, Rice with Peas and Pine Nuts, Lemon Buttered Vegetables are perfect with it. If you don't want to make Puff Pastry, you can now buy it, so just fill it with Custard. It is a natural to go with the Lamb Chops.

Oven Browned Potato Chunks

Peel Idaho potatoes and cut into large chunks. Roll chunks in oil, (or use a non-stick spray), season with salt and pepper. Place in a pan under a broiler. Roast and turn until all sides are very well browned.

Broiled Lamb Rib Chops With Mint Jelly

Cut vertically down between the ribs of a crown roast of lamb, to produce rib chops. Trim the meat and fat from the rib ends. They are best when broiled either under direct heat, or in a heavy uncovered skillet. Rub chops on both sides with your favorite seasonings, and coat with melted butter. Dry mustard and a little ground cloves work well. (You may want to add chopped or crumbled dry mint or other herbs). To broil by direct heat, lay the chops on a cold greased rack and place over live coals, or under the broiler of your oven, fairly close to the heat, and sear on both sides. Lower the heat and finish cooking. Turn carefully and do not prick the brown crust. To pan broil, lay the chops in a sizzling hot skillet with melted butter, sear quickly on both sides, then turn the chops on edges and hold with tongs to brown the fat. Reduce heat, turn frequently, and finish cooking at a low temperature. Do not add water. Arrange them prettily on a platter, garnish with fresh parsley or sprigs of mint, and serve with mint jelly. (It is also possible to have double chops cut, 1½" to 2" thick.)

MINT JELLY:

Wash mint leaves and tender stems and pack a cup full. Add 1 cup water, ½ cup apple vinegar, and 3 ½ cups sugar. Boil in a fairly large pot. Stir to dissolve the sugar, and bring to a heavy boil. Add as much green vegetable coloring as you need in order to get the color you want. Add half a bottle of liquid pectin. Boil vigorously for about a minute. Skim and strain into glasses. Fill sterilized jars and seal.

Rice With Peas & Pine Nuts

Toast fresh pine nuts in a little butter until golden. Cook fresh or frozen garden peas until tender (the little petit pois will not hold up in this mixture). Season a pot of cooked rice with salt, pepper, and tarragon. Stir the peas into the pine nuts, add a little more butter, and stir the hot rice into the pot. Reheat just before serving.

Custard Filled Pastry Triangles

QUICK PUFF PASTE:

Use 1 cup bread flour, cut in 1 Tbsp. lard and ⅞ cups butter. Quickly stir in enough ice water to just moisten the dough and make it hold together. Roll out to a thickness you can handle, but not too thick, and cut into 4" squares. (If you want to make this really easy, buy already prepared puff paste at your grocery.) Put filling in the center, fold over, and crimp or press edges together. Bake in a hot oven (400 to 450 degrees) until light golden brown.

CREAM FILLING:

⅔	cup sugar
½	cup flour
⅛	tsp. salt
2	cups scalded milk
1	tsp. lemon extract (or almond or vanilla)
2	eggs, beaten lightly

Mix dry ingredients, add scalded milk gradually, and cook for 15 minutes in a double boiler, stirring constantly until mixture thickens. Add eggs and stir quickly. Cook for 3 minutes more. Cool and add lemon extract.

Have a cozy little supper for two in the breakfast nook, and serve up Hot Sausage and Sauerkraut, a dish from our German ancestors who settled in the South. All of our grandmothers made good rich Cheesy Potato Casseroles, and they go so well with the main dish. The meal doesn't need any more heavy food, so a simple salad and a light Lemon flavored Pound Cake serve very well to complete the menu.

Hot Sausage & Sauerkraut

Cut smoked sausage in large chunks. Heat in a small amount of water. It will begin to make its own grease. When sausage is well browned, pour off the excess grease and deglaze the pan with a little water or red wine. Add the drained sauerkraut and season with salt and pepper to taste. The browned sausage will improve the flavor of the sauerkraut. Heat until it is good and hot, adding water or wine if needed.

Cheesy Potato Casserole

Ingredients needed: 6 medium potatoes, butter/margarine, salt and pepper, flour and milk. Romano cheese is optional.

Pare and thinly slice 6 medium potatoes. (Some cooks now like the added flavor of the brown skin and do not remove it, but at least, scrub them well). Butter the baking dish and overlap the potatoes to cover the bottom of the dish. Season with salt and pepper and sprinkle some flour over the layer, but don't overdo it. Repeat this entire process for a second layer, but do not make a third layer. Pour in just enough milk to come almost to the top of the potatoes, but not quite. If you want, sprinkle Romano cheese on both layers. Dot the top with paprika. Bake in a 375 degree oven for 1 hour, or until potatoes are tender. If they start to brown too fast, lower the heat or cover with foil.

Cauliflower, Broccoli, & Carrot Sticks

Cook florets of cauliflower, broccoli, and short carrot sticks or baby carrots until barely tender. Melt a stick of butter in a heavy skillet over a medium low fire. Stir in 2 tsp. lemon juice, 1 tsp. grated lemon peel and 1 Tbsp. of finely chopped chives. Add salt and freshly ground black pepper. Put hot vegetables in a large bowl and pour lemon butter sauce over them.

Herbed Feta Cheese & Lettuce Salad

Toss torn pieces of iceberg lettuce and green leaf lettuce. Mix together thoroughly. Sprinkle with cubes of any white herbed cheese. A favorite is herb and garlic cheese, or use a pepper cheese. Serve with oil, vinegar, salt, and pepper. There are many flavored vinegars on the market that you may want to use. Raspberry vinegar gives a lovely tangy flavor.

Old Fashioned Pound Cake

1   Lb. butter (2 cups)
1   Lb. sifted cake flour (4 cups)
1   Lb. sugar (2 cups)
10 eggs, separated
1   tsp. vanilla

(You can see where the cake gets its name. I have never weighed the eggs to see if they make up a pound too.)

Cream the butter, until it is easily handled, and slowly work in the flour. It will have the consistency of meal. Cream together the egg yolks, sugar, and vanilla. Beat hard until thickened and foamy. Beat egg whites separately until pretty stiff, and fold into the first mixture. Then beat again for a few minutes. Make in two pans. Use loaf pans lined with wax paper, or use non stick loaf pans. The usual size is 4" X 8". Bake in a 325 degree oven until golden brown or about 1 hour and 20 minutes. For a variety, buy a jar of lemon curd from the store's jelly and jam department. Cut the cooled cake in two pieces, horizontally, from end to end. Spread the lemon curd between the two layers and over the top. You could also substitute lemon extract for vanilla in the cake, or make one of each.

Green Salad with Red Onion Rings

Slice red onions, as thin or thick as you like them, and marinate in balsamic vinegar overnight. Make a bed of Romaine or red lettuce, and lay onion rings on top. Dress with the following mixture.

2   hard boiled eggs
1   tsp. powdered mustard
    Salt & cayenne pepper
1   tsp. paprika
4   Tbsp. balsamic vinegar
2   Tbsp. honey
¼   cup minced celery
¼   cup toasted sesame seeds

Mash yolks of boiled eggs. Work dry mustard, salt, cayenne pepper, and paprika into the mashed yolks. Add the balsamic vinegar and honey and mix well. Stir in chopped celery. Toast sesame seeds in a little butter, in a heavy skillet until light brown. Add to dressing and stir. Chop whites of eggs into small bits, and stir into salad dressing, or if you prefer, save and sprinkle over the top of the salad.

*A*nother way to serve Pork Chops is to stuff thick fresh ones with Cornbread and Sausage Stuffing. This meal and its accompaniments will extend a warm welcome to your guests. The Fancy Rice is a version of a Rice Pilaf which has often been called "Rice Perloo" in the South, as in "Squirrel Rice Perloo." A nice light Fruit Salad and a great Bread Pudding covered with thick meringue will surely please your guests.

Sausage Stuffed Pork Chops

Have your butcher cut the pork chops about 1½" thick and then cut a pocket through the lean part and back to the bone. Stuff the pocket and fasten the opening with some sort of skewers. Rub with salt and pepper on the outside and then rub in a little flour. Sear both sides rapidly in a well greased, hot, heavy pan. Place the chops on a rack with a pan under it, in a 350 degree oven. Cover the pan with aluminum foil. The chops should be cooked and tender in 50 minutes or less. Remove the skewers before serving.

Cornbread & Sausage Stuffing

Brown a package of bulk sausage in a frying pan. Break it up as it cooks, until it all crumbles apart, with no lumps in it. A chopped onion should be added about halfway through. Drain off all the grease. Use a package of bread stuffing mix and add the recommended amount of hot water. (Cornbread stuffing may also be used). If the stuffing is not seasoned, add a little thyme and sage. Stir a well beaten egg into the stuffing, and then blend the browned sausage and onions in.

Fancy Rice

Put 2 cups of long grained rice in 2 quarts of boiling water. Add salt, 1 Tbsp. vinegar, and 1 Tbsp. oil. Drain in a colander for 18 minutes. It will be nice and fluffy. Lightly brown 1 chopped onion in butter in a large skillet, plus 1 chopped yellow pepper and ½ cup of chopped pecans or walnuts. Remove from heat and add ½ cup raisins that have been soaked in warm water and drained. Stir the cooked rice into the mixture in the skillet. Reheat, while still mixing, and serve as soon as possible.

Mixed Fruit Salad

Mix large cubes of cantaloupe with sweet red seedless grapes, oranges, and grapefruit sections. Use fresh sections of the citrus fruit, or buy the refrigerated jars rather than using canned sections or mandarin oranges. Serve with poppy seed dressing on curly green leaf lettuce.

Bread Pudding with Meringue

3   cups torn pieces of stale bread, toasted (or very dry)
½   cup raisins
1   pt. milk
3   egg yolks, well beaten
½   cup sugar
1   tsp. vanilla
2   Tbsp. melted butter
⅓   tsp. salt
2   cups fresh or canned peaches

Drain canned peaches well. Place bread in a baking dish and sprinkle raisins over the top. Bring milk to a simmer. Beat egg yolks until foamy, stir in sugar, vanilla, melted butter, and salt. Pour this mixture carefully over bread and raisins. Set baking dish in a pan with about 1" of hot water in it. Bake at 325 degrees until top is lightly browned. (French bread works very well for this recipe).

MERINGUE TOPPING: Beat 3 egg whites until foamy. Add ¼ tsp. cream of tarter and beat again. Gradually add 3 Tbsp. sugar and ½ tsp. vanilla. Continue beating until peaks form. Spread carefully over the pudding, pulling up little peaks across the top. Place under oven broiler until lightly browned, but not too close to the broiler element.

Set an inviting table in a homey atmosphere by the brick fireplace. Enjoy the quilted handwork hanging above it. Pork Tenderloin is so easy to fix, especially with this Spicy Sauce Recipe. Herbed Rice and Baby Yellow Squash will not detract from the fine flavor of the tenderloin. Pour Thousand Island Dressing generously over Wedges of Iceberg Lettuce, and serve Blueberry Scones and Fruit and Nut Bread.

Dressed Iceberg Lettuce

Peel off loose or torn leaves on the outside of a compact head of iceberg lettuce. Cut into quarters with base attached at bottom. This will hold everything together. Cut each quarter into 2 or 3 wedges, depending on the size of the head. Serve each piece on its side, with a healthy amount of dressing poured over it.

Thousand Island Dressing:

Add 1 Tbsp. each of chili sauce, sweet pickle relish, chopped olives and chopped pimento to 1 cup of mayonnaise. (1 Tbsp. each of chopped bell pepper and celery may be added if you like.) Chill well before using.

Baby Yellow Squash

6   small yellow squash
½   small sweet onion, finely
    chopped
3   leaves of basil, finely chopped
1   Tbsp. butter
    Sprinkle of bacon bits

Clip the green stem end off of
each squash. Cut into small
chips. Melt butter in a pan. Add
all ingredients with a pinch of
salt. The flavor of these vegetables is so delicate that it should
not be spoiled with too much
seasoning. Cutting it into the
small chips makes it blend
together in a creamy mixture
and improves the flavor. Cook
gently until just tender.

Herbed Rice

2   cups long grained rice
2   qts. water
1   cup chopped, green onion tops
1   Tbsp. butter
½   cup chopped parsley
    A few leaves of fresh basil,
    finely chopped
    Salt & pepper to taste

Bring at least a quart of water to
a boil, add rice and bring to a
boil again. Lower heat and cook
for 18 minutes. Put 1 Tbsp. each
of oil and vinegar in the water. It
will make the rice come out nice
and fluffy and the oil will keep it
from boiling over. Drain in a
colander. While the rice is draining, lightly cook all the greens in
the butter. Turn the rice into the
skillet with the onions and herbs,
stir together thoroughly, and
keep hot until serving time.

Sauced Roast
Pork Tenderloin

Tie the tenderloin together at
several places. Mix and blend ½
tsp. each of salt, chili powder,
and garlic salt. Rub the mixture
into the tenderloin on all sides.
Place tenderloin in a baking dish.
Set it in a 325 degree oven for 3
minutes. Remove from oven,
pour well stirred sauce over it,
and replace it in the oven.
Continue baking for about 30 to
40 minutes, until done, basting it
at regular intervals.

SPICY SAUCE:

Microwave the following ingredients in a 2 cup measuring cup or
a glass bowl of equal size: ½ cup
apple jelly, ½ cup ketchup, 1
Tbsp. vinegar, and ½ tsp. chili
powder. Heat on high for 1
minute. Let stand in the
microwave for 1 minute.

Blueberry Scones

1   cup blueberries
2   cups cake flour
2   tsp. baking powder
¼   cup sugar
½   tsp. salt
4   Tbsp. butter
1   orange
1   cup heavy cream

Mix together dry ingredients.
Add butter to mixture with the
help of a pastry blender or fork
until crumbly. Scrape the zest
from the orange and chop fine.
Add the blueberries and orange

zest. Mix until berries are well
distributed. Add cream and mix
until you have a good, manage-
able dough. Shape into a ball.
Knead a few times on a floured
surface. Divide into two balls and
pat each out into rounds, ½" to
¾" thick. Cut each into 6 or 8 triangles. Bake on ungreased baking
sheet in a 400 degree oven until
lightly browned, about 20 minutes or more. Serve warm.

Fruit & Nut Bread

1½ cups dried apricots (or other
    dried fruit)
1½ cups boiling water
2   Tbsp. butter
¾   cup sugar
1   tsp. salt
2   eggs, well beaten

SIFT TOGETHER:

1   cup whole wheat flour
1½ cups pastry flour
1   tsp. soda
1   cup almonds, chopped
    (Walnuts, pecans, or other
    nuts may be used)

Run apricots through food
processor until well cut up. Add
next 4 ingredients and let cool.
Add all other ingredients. Grease
2 small loaf pans, dust well with
flour. Turn the mixture into the
pans. Bake 1 hour or longer in a
350 degree oven. Check to see if
they are browning and pulling
away from the sides of the pans.

Baby Back Ribs are perfect for dining al fresco, and Beans flavored with Barbecue Sauce are needed to go with the main course. Fix Baby Carrots for Finger Food, stuff Tomatoes with Egg Salad, and serve a good Potato Salad with it. To top it off, serve a Lemon Chess Pie.

Baby Back Ribs

1   Lb. baby back beef ribs
2   Tbsp. vegetable oil
3   Tbsp. chili sauce
2   Tbsp. balsamic vinegar
    Dash of black pepper
    Dash of dry mustard
    Dash of Worcestershire sauce
    Pinch of cloves

Wipe ribs and lay out separately in a roasting pan. Roast ribs at 425 degrees for about 10 minutes on each side. Prepare sauce by mixing all above ingredients. Remove ribs from oven and thoroughly brush all over with sauce. Return pan to oven and increase temperature to 450 degrees. Bake until ribs are tender for about 20 minutes. Baste with the rest of the sauce at intervals while baking. Reduce heat to 400 degrees for the last 10 minutes. If ribs are getting too brown, cover with aluminum foil.

Butter Beans

2   slices raw bacon, chopped (or ½ cup chopped ham)
½   medium onion, chopped
2½ cups fresh butter beans
4   cups water
    Salt & pepper

Fry bacon, drain, add onion and fry a little. Add water and beans to pot and boil until tender. Add seasoning as they cook. You may need to add water as the beans cook. If you like a little sauce, you can sprinkle in a little flour towards the end of the cooking time.

Tomatoes Filled with Egg Salad

Cut out tops of medium sized tomatoes and scoop out the inside with a teaspoon. Chop hard boiled eggs, and add mayonnaise, salt, and cayenne pepper. Chop ½ of a bell pepper, a few green onions, and mix with the eggs. Add sweet pickle relish and some Dijon mustard. Stuff the tomato shells. Serve on leaf lettuce.

Beans with Barbeque Sauce

1   Lb. red beans
2   Tbsp. vegetable oil
1   large onion, chopped
1   bell pepper, chopped
4   cloves garlic, minced
4   cups water
3   Tbsp. molasses
1   cup chili sauce
¼   cup Worcestershire sauce
2   tsp. dry mustard
¼   tsp. cayenne pepper
    Salt to taste

Soak beans overnight. Drain water off of beans and add 4 cups of water. Stir in all other ingredients. Cover and cook slowly until beans are tender and mixture is creamy - 3 to 4 hours. Add water as necessary. Obviously, the beans have not been barbecued over a pit, but they will taste great with the barbecued ribs.

Baby Carrot Finger Food

Cook baby carrots in water, with a little salt added, until tender. Roll in melted butter and then in seasoned bread crumbs. Arrange in a circle with tips in center and stem end out. Punch a small hole in the stem end with a skewer and put a sprig of flat leaved or curly parsley in each one.

Lemon Chess Pie

1   stick butter, melted
3   eggs, beaten
1½ cups sugar
2   Tbsp. flour
1   Tbsp. lemon juice
1   tsp. lemon zest
1   pie shell, unbaked

Preheat oven to 325 degrees. Mix all ingredients together, and pour into unbaked pie shell. Bake in a 400 degree oven for 15 minutes. Reduce heat to 350 degrees and bake for 20 to 30 minutes. Shake pie gently. It should be fairly firm and just quiver slightly. Cover the edges of the pie with strips of foil, and they won't get so brown and brittle.

Perhaps you have forgotten how good Smoked Pork Chops and Fried Apples taste. My Aunt used to let me stand on a stool and stir the apples while she watched the chops. She served Corn Dodgers, and also Glazed Carrots with them, because neither one of us cared for plain carrots. Hopping John is a good old country dish to serve with this country supper.

Hopping John

1	Lb. black eyed peas
8	ham hocks, (more may be used if desired)
1	large onion, chopped
¼	cup green onion tops
¼	cup chopped bell peppers
¼	cup parsley, chopped
2	bay leaves
	Salt and cayenne pepper to taste
¼	cup butter
2	cups rice

Wash peas, change water and bring to a rolling boil for a few minutes. Remove from heat and soak overnight in that same water, enough to cover the peas. In the morning bring to a boil again and add everything except butter and rice. Reduce heat and simmer for 3 hours. Peas should be creamy but remain whole. Add butter and mix well.

Put rice in 4 quarts boiling salted water to which 1 Tbsp. of oil and 1 Tbsp. of vinegar have been added. Reduce heat some and cook 18 minutes. Drain and rinse in colander. Return colander to rest over the pot which has had a little water put in it. Steam a few minutes until warmed through. Mix peas and rice and serve with ham hocks.

**Serve this on New Year's day to bring prosperity throughout the year. Serve cabbage also on this day and you will have money coming in all year.

Smoked Pork Chops

Trim extra fat from chops. Leave just enough fat for them to fry well. Heat a large heavy frying pan until it is good and hot. Place chops in the pan, putting the side with the most fat down. Brown on both sides. Reduce heat, cover tightly, and continue frying until they are thoroughly cooked, 30 to 40 minutes. Do not add water until absolutely necessary. Turn over as you need to.

Corn Dodgers

Mix ½ tsp. salt with 4 cups white cornmeal, and cut in 1 Tbsp. butter flavored shortening with a pastry cutter. Add 2 cups buttermilk and stir well. Shape into small oblong "dodgers" with your hands and bake on a greased griddle in a hot oven.

Glazed Carrots

Melt 1 Tbsp. of butter in ½ cup of orange juice and add 1 Tbsp. of honey to the pan. Cook baby carrots in this sauce until tender, and salt lightly. Stir in 1 tsp. of cornstarch and continue cooking until slightly thickened. If you wish, sprinkle a little nutmeg in the sauce.

Fried Apples

Use 6 firm medium sized apples. Core, but do no peel. Cut in wedges, about ½" thick. Melt 1 cup butter in a large pan, add apples and cook for about 10 minutes. Sprinkle 1 cup of sugar over the apples and continue cooking, stirring occasionally, until transparent. Serve hot. This is the perfect accompaniment for fried pork chops.

Outdoor Picnics in the shade of the trees, need foods with zest. Spicy Meatloaf and some Sweet and Sour Red Cabbage both fill the bill. So do Zucchini and Tomatoes with Onions, Summer Treat Cole Slaw, and richly flavored Spiced Sherried Fruit. Serve Mushrooms stuffed with Crabmeat as an appetizer, and enjoy!

Spicy Meatloaf

1	sweet onion
1	green bell pepper
3	cups lean ground beef
2	eggs, lightly beaten
1	Tbsp. parsley
1	tsp. basil or oregano
1	cup seasoned bread crumbs
1	cup milk
1	large can tomato sauce
1	Tbsp. Worcestershire sauce
1	tsp. salt
2	Tbsp. melted butter

Chop onion and pepper. Mix ground beef and lightly beaten eggs. Add the onions, pepper, and herbs and stir in thoroughly. Add the bread crumbs and milk alternately. Stir in ½ of the tomato sauce and the Worcestershire sauce, salt and melted butter. Press into a greased pyrex loaf pan. (If the mixture seems too liquid and soft, stir in more bread crumbs before you do this.) Spread the other half of the tomato sauce over the top, sprinkle bread crumbs lightly over this, and add a few pats of butter on the top. Bake in a 350 degree oven for 30 to 40 minutes until the top is nice and crusty.

Zucchini & Tomatoes with Onion

Wash tomatoes and zucchini and cut into chunks, but not too large. Chop half an onion and cook in a little butter and olive oil until golden. Add tomatoes and zucchini. Season with salt, pepper, basil, and parsley. Simmer until tender, but not too soft. A little red wine can be added if desired.

Stuffed Mushrooms

Wipe fresh mushrooms carefully with a damp cloth; don't wash unless you have to. Break off the stems and chop them up. Chop onions fine. Cook onions in butter, with the chopped stems. Add a dash of Worcestershire sauce, some bread crumbs, and a small can of crabmeat. Mix until thick enough to handle, stuff caps with the mixture, and bake in a little melted butter until browned and juicy. This is quick and easy to prepare.

Summer Treat Cole Slaw

Shred cabbage finely and fill a large bowl. Add 2 Tbsp. vinegar, 2 Tbsp. sugar, and a little salt and pepper. Stir well. Cover the bowl and place in the refrigerator overnight. Your cole slaw will be much better if you give it time to marinate in this sweet and sour mixture. The next morning, drain a small can of crushed pineapple, (or a large can, depending on how much you like), and mix the pineapple and some chopped peanuts into the cole slaw. Add mayonnaise and some half and half cream. So much of this recipe is a matter of individual preference, so taste as you go and add as much of each ingredient as it suits you. The salad should be creamy with a sweet and sour flavor. Adding the peanuts gives it a new and delicious flavor. (If it is too sweet, add "sour," and vice versa).

Spiced Sherried Fruit

Drain the following fruits: Canned apricot halves, peach slices, baby pears (or pear quarters), spiced crabapples, pineapple chunks, plums and papaya chunks (canned or refrigerated). Add enough brandy to heat the fruit in, moving it around gently until all is well heated. Serve hot, in bowls or compotes. Add your favorite spices such as cinnamon, allspice, nutmeg or ginger, or any combination thereof.

Sweet & Sour Red Cabbage

¼ stick butter
1 red onion, sliced thin
2 Granny Smith apples, peeled and sliced
1 small head red cabbage
½ cup Burgundy wine
¼ cup brown sugar
¼ cup balsamic vinegar
2 tsp. dark mustard
   Salt & red pepper to taste

Cut the cabbage in quarters and remove the hard core. Slice it thinly or put it through your processor. Melt the butter in a deep skillet, and put the onion and apple slices in the bottom of the pot. Add the thinly shredded cabbage and cook over a low fire, adding all other ingredients. Do not stir for awhile. As the ingredients begin to soften, start stirring at intervals, eventually bringing everything up from the bottom and mixing it well. Continue to cook slowly until everything in the pot is tender and blended. Add a little water as necessary. Check for seasoning near the end and correct with more salt and pepper if necessary. This recipe comes from our German ancestors and is a delicious and colorful dish to serve.

Beefy Macaroni Bake is a recipe which Southerners have adapted from the Italian cuisine. It is an old favorite and is full of tasty ingredients. It makes a hearty supper dish, after a hard days work. You don't need much to go with it, so serve a perky Vegetable Salad, some Garlic Toast, and Apple Brown Betty, which is another recipe from our grandmothers.

Beefy Macaroni Bake

Cook ½ pkg. of elbow macaroni in salted boiling water until just tender. Cook 1 chopped onion and 1 diced bell pepper until soft. Set aside. Brown 1 Lb. of lean ground beef, add 1 can of stewed tomatoes or tomato sauce, and cook down. Season with basil or oregano, or both, and a little Worcestershire sauce. Stir in onions, bell pepper, 1 cup shredded cheddar cheese and the macaroni. Pour into a large casserole dish and bake in a 350 degree oven until hot and bubbly.

Toasted French Bread with Garlic Spread

Cut a loaf of French bread in half lengthwise, and then cut pieces about 3" long. Crush a few cloves of garlic, throw out the skin, and mix with softened butter. Spread the bread with the garlic butter and toast in the oven. Serve immediately.

Marinated Vegetable Salad

Simmer sliced carrots and zucchini until tender. Cook broccoli and cauliflower florets until you can stick a fork in them. Nothing should be too soft. Drain well and put into a bowl together. Mix in oil and vinegar or Russian dressing and toss well. Chill overnight. Serve on lettuce with pieces of purple kale or red cabbage leaves tucked in among the lettuce and chilled vegetables.

Apple Brown Betty

1	stick butter, melted
2	cups bread crumbs
2	cups sliced apples
	Cinnamon, ground
½	cup apple juice
½	cup brown sugar
	Juice and grated rind of one lemon

Put a layer of apple slices on the bottom of a baking dish. Sprinkle buttered crumbs over the apples. Sprinkle the top of the layer with brown sugar and cinnamon. Sprinkle a little lemon juice and ground lemon rind on top. Repeat layers until dish is filled. Finish with a layer of crumbs and pour the apple juice over the top. A few pats of butter can be placed on the top. Cover with foil and bake at 300 degrees for 30 minutes. Remove the cover and bake 45 minutes longer.

A *country lunch in a room with a view, requires Country Fried Steaks, Cream Gravy, and Hashed Brown Potatoes. Add Butter Beans, Spiced Apples, and Blackberry Cobbler, and then relax, eat well, and enjoy the calm scenery. Decorate the table with sprays of white pear blossom's or some other "airy fairy" twigs of flowers.*

Country Fried Steaks

Ingredients needed: 1 large beef round, not too thick, salt, pepper, flour, and milk.

Cut round into separate steaks. Sprinkle salt, pepper, and flour onto each steak and pound with a heavy meat mallet. Turn over and repeat process on the other side. Brown both sides in bacon drippings or cooking oil. Place on a platter and keep warm.

CREAM GRAVY:

Add milk and a little salt and pepper to the pan and deglaze the brown drippings. Thicken slightly with a mixture of flour and water. Simmer until flour is well cooked. Serve the meat with this cream gravy.

Hash Browned Potatoes

Boil 4 medium potatoes until barely tender. Cool and chop coarsely. Place in a mixing bowl. Mix with ½ cup chopped onion, ⅓ cup milk, 3 Tbsp. flour, salt, and pepper to taste. Heat about 4 Tbsp. of oil in a heavy skillet (black iron is best). Add potatoes and brown on one side, then turn over to brown the other side.

Blackberry Cobbler

Make pie dough for a two crust pie, or use prepared folded pie crust in a box. Roll out and place half of it in the bottom of a 9" X 9" pyrex dish. Fill with a berry filling, whatever is in season. Top with the other half of the crust. Brush on melted butter and sprinkle with sugar. Bake in 400 degree oven for about 30 minutes, until nicely browned.

FILLING: Mix 1 cup sugar and 1 Tbsp. corn starch in a 2 quart saucepan. Add 1 cup water, stirring until smooth. Boil about 3 minutes, add 3 cups fresh or frozen berries. Pour into pie crust.

**Don't worry if the filling bubbles up over the top crust. It only makes people hungrier for it. Some people like to use a biscuit dough topping. (See page 23 for Shortcake Sweet Biscuit Dough for recipe.)

Spiced Apples

6   medium to small firm apples, peeled and cored
1   cup sugar
1   Tbsp. lemon juice
    Red food coloring
2   6 oz. cans apple juice
1   4 oz. pkg. hot cinnamon candies

Put the apples in a pot just large enough to let them all sit on the bottom. Put a dash of lemon juice in the apple juice. As you peel and core the apples, dip them in the juice, to moisten all around, top and bottom, so they won't turn brown while paring and coring the others. Put all the ingredients in and add water until it comes ⅔ of the way up the sides of the apples. Bring to a boil, lower heat, but continue at a bubbly simmer. Stir as candies melt. Turn apples over every so often. Add the food coloring while they cook, drop by drop, until the water is red enough. The liquid will make a syrup which will put a nice glaze on the apples. Don't take them out until they glisten and look a little translucent on the surface.

For a Midsummer's Eve on the patio, on a bright flowered table-cloth, serve a fine Roast Beef with Yorkshire Pudding as our English ancestors served it. Try this fantastic recipe for Ethereal Potatoes with it. Serve Brussels Sprouts, and Cherry Gelatin Salad. A meringue pie is always a great treat, so serve a delicious Lemon Meringue Pie.

Ethereal Potatoes

You will need about 2 Lbs. of potatoes. Preheat the oven to 350 degrees, prick the skins of the potatoes with a fork, and rub them with oil. They should be tender in about 1 hour. (You can do this in the microwave, but they tend to get too dry). Peel the potatoes when cool enough to handle, and mash thoroughly. Soften 2 sticks of butter and mash into the potatoes. Beat 6 eggs well and whip them into the potatoes, a little at a time. Salt and pepper to your taste, and add some grated nutmeg. Finally, add at least ½ cup of whipping cream, as much as it takes to make the potatoes wonderfully creamy. Spoon the whole mixture into an oven proof dish, sprinkle some bacon bits over the top and then some melted butter. Bake for 25 minutes. Raise the heat to 400 degrees during the last 5 minutes.

Roast Beef with Yorkshire Pudding

Rub rump roast with salt and pepper. Cut slits here and there and insert small cloves or pieces of garlic. Place meat on a rack, with fat side up, and a pan under it to catch the drippings. If there is no fat, you can lay strips of bacon over the top of the roast. Do not add water or cover pan. Insert a meat thermometer into the center of the roast. It should get up to between 150 - 170 degrees when roast is done. Roast 25 to 30 minutes per pound. Slice into roast as soon as you remove it from the oven so it does not continue to cook.

YORKSHIRE PUDDING

1 cup flour
½ tsp. salt
1 cup milk
2 eggs
Pan drippings from the roast-beef

Mix flour and salt. Combine milk and eggs, add to flour, and beat well until smooth. Pour hot drippings from the roast, into a hot shallow pan to a depth of 1". Pour mixture in quickly and bake in 400 degree oven for ½ hour. The pudding may be placed in the pan with the roast beef and left for 15 minutes to catch the juices from the roast. Serve on a platter with the roast.

Lemon Buttered Brussels Sprouts

Take off any wilted leaves and let the Brussels sprouts soak in lukewarm water, lightly salted. Trim the stem end and cut an X in each stem end before you put them in the water. Drain. Bring salted water to a boil, and drop Brussels sprouts in together with an onion, 2 short stalks of celery, a few peppercorns, 2 sprigs of tarragon, and a bay leaf. Add ¼ cup of lemon juice and pieces of lemon peel (with no white). Drain again. Heat ¼ cup butter and gently stir sprouts in it over a low heat until they are barely browned. Keep hot and serve as soon as possible.

Lemon Meringue Pie

¾ cup sugar
¾ cup boiling water
2 Tbsp. cornstarch
2 Tbsp. flour
2 egg yolks
3 Tbsp. lemon juice
1 grated lemon rind
1 tsp. butter

Mix cornstarch, sugar, and flour then pour the boiling water over the mixture. Stir constantly. Cook until thick. Add egg yolks, butter, lemon juice and rind. Cook until egg thickens. Stir constantly, as mixture will burn readily. Fill baked crust, cover with meringue, and brown in oven.

MERINGUE

Beat 3 egg whites with ¼ tsp. salt. Beat in 6 Tbsp. sugar and ½ tsp. vanilla. Spread on pie with a spatula, sealing edges, and pull it up in little peaks here and there. Put it in a 475 degree oven, or under the broiler, until light brown, about 4 minutes.

Cherry Gelatin Salad

Drain 2 cans of seedless dark cherries, but save the juice. Add ½ cup of cherry wine to the juice and then add water to make 4 cups of liquid. Bring the liquid to a boil, pour over 2 packages (or one large) of dark cherry Jello. Stir until completely dissolved and place in refrigerator. When it begins to thicken, and is almost set, stir the cherries into it. If you put them in at the beginning, they will all rise to the top, and you want them to be distributed throughout the gelatin. Serve on lettuce with a dollop of mayonnaise.

*H*ow about a Convertible Pepper Supper? You could amuse your guests and buy different colored peppers to stuff, and switch the tops to make a kaleidoscope of colors on the platter. If you fry Lye Hominy the right way, with Ham Bits, it is quite tasty. With Vegetables and Cucumbers in Mint Sauce, everyone will be happy. The best dessert with all this, will be Toasted Angel Food Cake with a thick Raspberry Sauce poured over it.

Cauliflower, Broccoli & Cheese

Break broccoli and cauliflower into florets and drop into boiling water. Remove them when they are barely tender. Heat 1 can of creamy onion soup (which is a lot easier than making a white sauce and adding chopped onions to it). Add 1 cup cooked rice, ½ cup grated cheddar cheese, and ½ tsp. thyme. Stir to blend. When it starts to get hot and bubbly, add as much milk as it needs and stir in the broccoli and cauliflower florets. Add pepper. The soup should provide enough salt. Before serving, bake in a casserole until bubbly and crusty. Topping with bread crumbs and pats of butter is optional.

Cucumbers in Mint Sauce over Lettuce

Peel 2 or 3 cucumbers, split down the center, and remove the seeds. You can leave narrow strips of green skin on the outside if you wish. It adds a little color. Cut into small chips, salt lightly, and let the chips stand in a colander to draw water and drain. Chop some mint into very small pieces and stir into a small carton of sour cream. When cucumbers have finished draining, pat them with paper towels and stir them into the sour cream. Let stand in the refrigerator, preferably overnight. Add a little white pepper if you wish. Serve on a bed of crisp lettuce.

Angel Food Cake with Raspberry Sauce

Make or buy an angel food cake. One baked in a loaf pan is best, but a round one is alright. Slice into square slices or wedge shaped pieces with a serrated bread knife. Just before serving, toast the slices in the oven on both sides. It should be a nice golden brown, but watch it carefully. Serve each slice on a dessert plate and pour raspberry sauce over the top. To make the sauce, use 1 pkg. or more of frozen raspberries with the juice. Warm slightly. Add a little sugar if necessary and stir in 1 tsp. of cornstarch to thicken it. Let it simmer long enough to see if it is thick enough. If not, add a little more cornstarch. If too thick, add a little apple, orange, or raspberry juice. The toasting caramelizes the sugar in the cake a little and really enhances the flavor of the cake. In addition, the cake does not get soggy from the sauce.

Fried Lye Hominy with Ham Bits

Melt ¼ cup of butter. Drain 2 cans of hominy and rinse in a colander. Fry small pieces of ham and add the drained hominy. Salt and pepper, and continue to fry until it begins to brown a little and pop and crackle. This takes away that slight soapy taste that the liquid of canned hominy tends to have.

Stuffed Peppers with Changeable Tops

Buy 2 each of red, yellow, and green bell peppers. Wash, cut the tops off, and save them. Clean the seeds and ribs out of the bottoms. Put them, tops and bottoms, in boiling water for just a minute to parboil, but don't let them get soft. Drain and cool.

STUFFING:

½   Lb. ground meat
2   Tbsp. butter
1   small onion, chopped
1   can corn niblets
½   cup milk
1   egg, beaten
1   cup seasoned stuffing mix
½   tsp. thyme
    Salt and Pickapeppa sauce
    to taste

Melt the butter in a skillet and brown the meat. When meat is about halfway done, add onions and corn niblets and continue cooking. When all are done, add milk and rapidly stir in the beaten egg. Add 1 cup of the stuffing mix and seasonings, and mix well. Place in a pan. Put lids on, but put a green lid on a red pepper, and a yellow one on green, etc. Bake 15 minutes in a 350 degree oven and then 10 minutes at 400 degrees.

J̶ust be "plain folks in the kitchen." Make a Cheese-Noodle Ring, and fill it up with Meatballs you have cooked in a brown gravy. Set it on the kitchen table with the beautiful Ruby Tomato Aspic, Asparagus with Mustard Cream Sauce, and big Buttermilk Biscuits. Cover 2 layers of Chocolate Cake with Marshmallow Cream, and give the family a real treat.

Meatballs & Gravy in a Cheese-Noodle Ring

1   Lb. lean ground beef
1   egg beaten
½   cup bread crumbs
1   small onion, chopped
½   tsp. oregano
¼   cup chopped parsley
     Salt and red pepper to taste
2   Tbsp. olive oil

Mix beef and all ingredients thoroughly, except oil. Form into small balls. Roll in flour and cook in hot oil, moving them around in order to brown them on all sides. Add a little water or beef stock and it will make just enough gravy to coat the balls and keep them moist. Grease an aluminum ring mold. Boil 2 cups of egg noodles until tender, and drain well. Beat an egg into ½ cup of milk. Stir the cooked noodles into this with a cup of shredded cheddar cheese. Spoon this mixture into a greased ring mold and press down well. Bake in a 350 degree oven until it is well melted together and bubbly. Remove from oven, run a knife around the edges of the mold, and turn out onto a dish with a rim, or a wide shallow bowl. Place the meatballs and gravy in the center of the ring and serve hot.

Asparagus with Mustard Cream Sauce

Buy slender young stalks of fresh asparagus. Hold a stalk in one hand, partway up from the bottom. Grasp the bottom with the other hand and quickly bend it. It will snap off at the point where it ceases to be tender, so throw the bottom away. You can steam them standing upright in a narrow pot, or lay them across the bottom of a large flat colander or steamer tray, and steam them over water on a medium heat for about 10 minutes. Salt lightly. Serve with a sauce.

MUSTARD CREAM SAUCE:

Melt 4 Tbsp. of butter and slowly blend in 4 Tbsp. flour over a low heat. Add the milk, a little at a time. Beat egg lightly and whip it into the sauce. Add 1 tsp. of dry mustard powder and a dash of lemon juice. Place the long spears of asparagus lengthwise on a platter, and pour the hot sauce across the middle of the stems. Dust with paprika.

Chocolate Cake with Marshmallow Cream

This is a "tasty quicky." Bake your favorite chocolate box cake in two layers. Let them cool thoroughly. Buy a jar of thick marshmallow cream. Soften if just a little in warm water, or remove the metal top, cover it, and zap it in the microwave for 10 minutes or so. Spread some on the first well cooled layer, which you have placed on a serving dish. Put the second layer on top of the first, and spread the rest of the cream on that. It will tend to run down the sides a little, but the taste is fantastic. Decorate it with a few maraschino cherries. Keep it in the refrigerator until serving time.

Buttermilk Biscuits

2	cups flour
3	Tbsp. butter
¼	tsp. baking soda
⅔-¾	cup milk
2	Tbsp. baking powder
1	tsp. salt

Combine all ingredients, cutting butter into the sifted dry ingredients. On floured board, knead gently, and roll lightly into ½" thickness. Cut with biscuit cutter dipped in flour. Bake in ungreased baking pan in 450 degree oven for 12 to 15 minutes.

Ruby Tomato Aspic

2	3 oz. pkg. of red raspberry Jello
2	cups boiling water
2	16 oz. cans plain stewed tomatoes
2	small packets of Knox Gelatin, softened in cold water
2	Tbsp. horseradish mustard
4	Tbsp. lemon juice
1	tsp. Tabasco
	Salt to taste
1	cup pecans, chopped into small pieces (optional)
1	cup sliced pimento olives (optional) Individual gelatin molds or one large ring mold

Dissolve Jello in the boiling water. Add the softened Knox Gelatin and the tomatoes (which have been run through the food processor to chop into small pieces). Cool in refrigerator. This recipe should fill at least 6 or 8 individual molds, depending on the size, or one large mold. If you add either the nuts or sliced pimento olives, or both, wait until the gelatin has begun to set up, and stir them in. Otherwise they will all float to the top. Do this in a large bowl, and then pour into the molds. If you spray the inside of the molds lightly with Pam or something similar, the gelatin will come out of the mold more easily.

*S*et a small table prettily, with dainty plates, for a small luncheon, and serve little Red Hot Meat Pies and gourmet Black Beans with Anisette. Include some tasty Tomatoes and Okra with Onions, a rich Potato Salad, and Cornbread. Add the surprise of a Black Bayou Spice Cake topped with whipped cream and swirled chocolate syrup.

Red Hot Meat Pies

2   Tbsp. oil
1   Lb. lean ground beef
1   small onion, chopped
1   bell pepper, chopped
¼   cup chopped parsley
2   Tbsp. Worcestershire sauce
1   Tbsp. lemon juice
¼   cup flour
    Salt and Tabasco sauce to taste

Use fresh or frozen folded pie crust. Thaw, if necessary, unfold carefully, and cut circles the size of a saucer. Press the trimmings of the dough together, reroll it, and cut more. Mix the meat and all of the other ingredients together. Place 2 Tbsp. of it on one side of each circle of dough, leaving the edges clear. Dampen the edges, fold over, and press down all around the curved edges with a fork. Fry in deep fat until golden, or brush with melted butter and bake at 350 degrees, for 30 minutes, or until browned. If you want to lessen the fat, spray with one of the baking sprays, before you put it in the oven.

Tomatoes & Okra with Onions

Wash 1 Lb. of young, tender okra, drain and slice. Chop a large onion rather fine. Wash and cut up 3 large tomatoes. Cook okra in 2 Tbsp. of olive oil until seeds turn pink. (This gets rid of the slimy part). Add onions during the end of the cooking time. When the mixture is fairly dry, add coarsely chopped tomatoes (and a little garlic if you wish). As the tomatoes cook, add salt, pepper, a little Worcestershire sauce, and a little vinegar. When this mixture is well cooked down, it almost becomes a meat substitute.

Black Beans Anisette

Soak 2 cups of black beans overnight. Drain in the morning, add more water and start cooking them, adding ¼ stick of butter, which helps to keep them creamy, and a little water as necessary. Add 1 onion, chopped, 2 bay leaves, 1 tsp. tarragon, and ½ tsp. anise seed (or a little anise oil, or some anisette liqueur). The anise suits the black beans well, but don't make it too strong. Add salt and cayenne pepper to taste. While the beans are cooking, cut 8 strips of bacon into 1" pieces. Fry a little and drain off the fat. Put the partially cooked bacon into the beans. Cook until the beans are creamy and tender.

Black Bayou Spice Cake

½   cup butter, softened
2   cups brown sugar
2   tsp. cinnamon
1   tsp. ginger
½   tsp. ground cloves
1   tsp. nutmeg
1   Tbsp. hot water
3   eggs, separated
2   cups cake flour
¼   tsp. salt
1   tsp. baking soda
1   cup sour cream

Cream butter and brown sugar together. Blend all the spices in a small bowl and moisten with 1 Tbsp. of hot water. Cream them into the mixture with the beaten egg yolks until thoroughly mixed. Beat until well aerated and fluffy. Add the flour and sour cream alternately, and beat well after each addition. Beat egg whites until stiff, but still moist, and then carefully fold them into the mixture. Bake in a preheated 350 degree oven for 50 minutes, in 2 layers, in 8" round pans. (You may also use a spice cake box mix if you feel lazy). After the layers have cooled completely, spread whipped cream or Cool Whip between the 2 layers and on the top. Finally, swirl thick chocolate sauce over the top.

*S*pend a lazy morning in bed, with a French Toast and Cheese Grits breakfast on a bedside table. You may have the choice of a Coddled Egg, English Muffins with Cream Cheese, a Boysenberry and Banana Fruit Cup, Orange Marmalade, and Strawberry or Blueberry Jam. Enjoy the comfort of Hot Coffee with Hot Milk. It's so nice to be lazy on a morning when you don't have to rush around.

French Toast

1   egg
½   tsp. salt
    Pepper to taste
4   Tbsp. milk
    Sliced day old bread, left out
    to air dry

Beat egg with milk, dip 3/8" slices of stale bread in the batter. Lift up and drain for a few seconds, and fry in a little margarine until brown on both sides. Serve with jelly, syrup, or granulated or powdered sugar. (Multiply ingredients, depending on how many people you are serving.)

English Muffins

½   cup scalded milk
1   cup water
1   tsp. salt
1   tsp. sugar
1   yeast cake dissolved in 1
    Tbsp. lukewarm water
3   Tbsp. shortening
4   cups bread flour

Cool milk to lukewarm, add water, salt, sugar, dissolved yeast cake, and 2 cups flour. Beat well. Let rise until double in bulk. Place on a lightly floured board. Flatten with a rolling pin to ¾" thickness. Let stand until light. Cut with a 2 ½" cutter (or use a tuna fish can with both ends cut out.) Bake 15 minutes on a hot buttered griddle, turning several times during cooking. Previously cut out muffins may be kept in the refrigerator until you want to bake them.

Coddled Eggs

Puncture larger end of each egg with an egg pricker, or needle. Place eggs in a pot, not too many at a time, and fill pot with enough water to cover eggs. It is a good idea to leave them out long enough to bring them to room temperature before you cook them. Gradually bring water to the boiling point. Reduce heat. Keep the water just below the boiling point and cook eggs for 5 minutes. Cut off heat and leave eggs in it for another 5 minutes. Pour off hot water and serve in an egg cup or a small bowl.

Cheese Grits

Cook 1 cup of grits in 1 quart boiling salted water, until thickened and tender. Remove from heat and add 8 oz. of grated cheddar cheese and 1 stick of butter. Pour into a greased casserole and bake in a 350 degree oven for 20 minutes.

Hot "Coffee Milk"

Have a pot of very hot, strong, dark coffee and an equal amount of hot milk ready. Pour equal amounts into each coffee cup. (Heat the milk until tiny bubbles appear around the edge, but do not let either the coffee or the milk boil. It will spoil the taste).

Boysenberry & Banana Fruit Cup

Use canned or frozen boysenberries, or any other kind of berries. Slice bananas. Put enough juice in to partially cover the bananas. You should not need to add sugar unless the berries are very tart. If you need it, I would suggest powdered sugar.

*F*or a really hearty brunch, try our Sunrise Casserole, which includes most everything you need in the morning, sausage, eggs, and grits. Hopping John makes another sturdy dish. Fix a beautiful Fruit Cup and make some Corn Pones available. Mix up a quick recipe for Easy Butter Icing and put a swirl on top of each piece of well browned Coffee Cake.

Sunrise Casserole

Fry 1 package of bulk sausage, stirring and breaking it up so that it becomes crumbly. Do not brown too much and dry it out. Let cool. Beat six eggs lightly. Add ½ cup chopped green bell pepper, ½ cup chopped green onion, with part of the tops, and 2 tsp. dry mustard. Measure 1 cup of seasoned croutons and add to the egg mixture. Then add 2 cups milk and 1 cup grated Cheddar cheese. Cook 2 packages of instant grits, adding enough water to keep them soft and not too thick. Add the sausage and grits to the egg mixture. Let the ingredients rest in an oven proof casserole dish - preferably overnight. Bake in a 350 degree oven for 40 to 50 minutes until nicely browned. Serve immediately and hot. Cut in squares to serve.

Fruit Bowl

Fill dessert bowls, sauce dishes, or sherbet glasses with pineapple wedges, cubes of cantaloupe, slices of kiwi fruit, pitted Bing cherries, and strawberries. You may use fresh, canned, or frozen Bing cherries. All pieces should be bite sized. If strawberries are large, cut them in half. Sprinkle with a little powdered sugar and garnish with a sprig of mint.

Coffee Cake with Butter Frosting Swirl

¼   cup butter flavored shortening
¾   cup sugar
2   eggs, separated
1   cup flour
2   tsp. baking powder
½   cup milk
¼   tsp. salt

Cream shortening and gradually work in the sugar. Beat the egg yolks into this mixture. Stir in the sifted dry ingredients and the milk alternately. Fold in the stiffly beaten egg whites carefully. Pour in a greased baking dish and bake at 350 degrees for 40 to 50 minutes until golden.

Butter Frosting

⅓   cup butter
1   cup confectioner's sugar
1   egg yolk
1   tsp. vanilla

Beat butter until creamy, add egg yolk, and beat in sugar gradually. Squeeze through a pastry tube for decorating.

*M*any Irish and Scottish people migrated to the South and brought certain traditions with them. You will find that St. Patrick's Day is well celebrated in many places. Corned Beef and Cabbage with Buttered Baby New Potatoes are appropriate dishes for the occasion. Make some Sweet Corn and Green Tomato Relish and decorate an Upside Down Cake with Pineapple Slices and Maraschino Cherries. Serve it on leafy green china and add a leprechaun to the bouquet.

Corned Beef & Cabbage

Use 4 Lbs. of corned beef and 1 large firm head of cabbage. Cover the meat with cold water, and cook it for 3 hours. Cut a head of cabbage into quarters and cut each quarter in half. At the end of 3 hours, add the cabbage to the pot and cook it until tender. Place the corned beef on a large serving platter and slice it into serving pieces. Place cabbage wedges in a bowl, or around the platter and drizzle melted butter over them.

Horseradish Sauce

    Tbsp. fresh horseradish
    Tbsp. vinegar
    tsp. dry mustard
    tsp. salt
    Dash of cayenne pepper
    tsp. paprika

Whip ½ cup of whipping cream and fold into above mixture of ingredients. A little tomato sauce may be added to this, if desired.

Buttered Baby New Potatoes

Pare a band around small new potatoes, leaving red skins on both ends. It makes a pretty pattern of color. Boil until tender, roll in melted butter, and sprinkle with chopped parsley. Salt and pepper if desired, or let your guests do their own.

Sweet Corn & Green Tomato Relish

2	ears of corn
2	cups chopped green tomatoes
2	pimentos, chopped
1	green bell pepper, chopped
3	cups rice vinegar
1	cup brown sugar
2	Tbsp. dry mustard
½	tsp. turmeric
1	Tbsp. salt
¼	cup flour

Cut the corn from the cob and scrape the milk out of the cob. Mix chopped vegetables with corn. Mix sugar, salt, turmeric, mustard, and flour with 1 cup cold vinegar. Heat 2 cups vinegar to the boiling point and add to cold vinegar and seasonings. Boil until mixture thickens. Add the corn and chopped vegetables and cook one half hour. Seal in hot sterilized jars.

Upside Down Cake

DO AHEAD: Melt 1/4 cup butter in a cake pan and add 1 cup brown sugar. Arrange drained pineapple slices in the pan and place a maraschino cherry in the center of each.

½	cup butter, softened
1	cup sugar
2	eggs, separated
½	cup milk
1¾	cups flour
½	tsp. salt
2	tsp. baking powder
½	tsp. vanilla

Reserve 1 Tbsp. sugar for each egg white to be used, and then work the remaining sugar into the butter. Beat together until light. Add beaten egg yolks to butter and sugar. Mix flour, salt, and baking powder. Add dry ingredients and liquid alternately, including vanilla. Beat thoroughly, but do not stir! Beat egg whites and sugar and fold them into the cake mixture. Pour into pan on top of pineapple slices. Bake at 375 degrees for 25 minutes, or until brown. Cool on rack, loosen the sides, and invert onto a serving platter.

*O*ne has to celebrate Easter with all the family rabbits and collected Easter eggs but also with Baked Ham and Sweet Potatoes topped with juicy pieces of Pineappl and Oranges, and with Baked Beans to go with the Ham. Of course, Boston Brown Bread was always served with Boston Baked Beans. Then please everyone with a Sour Cream Red Velvet Cake.

Boston Baked Beans

cups dried white beans
quart water
Lb. fat salt pork
tsp. salt
cup molasses
Tbsp. brown sugar
cup ketchup
cup chopped onions
cup boiling water
tsp. dry mustard

Cover beans with cold water and soak overnight. Drain and add 1 quart cold water. Bring to boil, but heat down, and simmer 2 hours. Add salt, molasses, sugar, ketchup and onions to the beans. Pour all into a greased baking dish with a cover. Press sliced pork in on the top, leaving rind exposed, and pour boiling water over it. Cover and bake slowly at 300 degrees for 4 or 5 hours.

Boston Brown Bread

cup white flour
cup cornmeal
cup coarse whole wheat flour
tsp. soda
tsp. salt
cup molasses
¾ cups milk
cup chopped walnuts

Stir and sift dry ingredients and mix well. Add other ingredients and stir again. Pour into greased molds (or tin cans) until they are ¾ full. Cover closely and steam in a colander for 2 hours. Remove cover and bake in a moderate 350 degree oven for 10 minutes, to dry.

Ham Steaks with Pineapple Rings

Melt enough butter or margarine in a pan to cover the bottom well. Place medium to large ham steaks (with most of the fat trimmed off) in the pan with some room left for pineapple slices. Fry the ham first, then add the pineapple. Lightly brown both ham and pineapple on both sides. Add the juice from the can of pineapple slices, and sprinkle some brown sugar over all. Let juice cook down, and sugar will begin to caramelize. Turn steaks and pineapple again so both sides will get the benefit of further browning. If pineapple rings begin to get too brown or soft, remove them to a platter. Serve both on the same platter.

Sour Cream Red Velvet Cake

1   cup thick sour cream
1   cup sugar
1   Tbsp. butter, melted
1½ cups flour
1   tsp. baking soda
½   tsp. salt
¼   cup red food coloring
⅔   cup cocoa
3   eggs
1   Tbsp. vanilla

Mix sour cream and sugar. Add melted butter. Make a paste of the food coloring and the cocoa. Add to the creamed mixture. Sift flour with baking soda and salt, and cream into cake. Break eggs into the mixture, add vanilla, and beat together very well.

ICING:

Cream together an 8 oz. pkg. of cream cheese, ½ cup soft butter, and 1 tsp. vanilla. Then cream in ½ cup sugar and beat vigorously to make the mixture light.

Sweet Potatoes with Orange & Pineapple Topping

4   large yams
2   Tbsp. brown sugar
¼   cup melted butter
¼   cup orange juice
1   small can pineapple chunks
1   jar fresh orange sections or
    Mandarin orange sections
    Mini marshmallows

Boil yams until tender. Peel, mash and mix with brown sugar, melted butter, and orange juice. Place mixture in a casserole dish, place pineapple chunks and orange sections on the top and sprinkle some of the mini marshmallows over the top. Place in 350 degree oven to reheat and brown marshmallows.

A Brace of Roasted Ducks in Orange Sauce makes a great presentation for a Christmas Dinner. Try a Fruited Bread Dressing for the Ducks, and fix Potato Puffs and Cauliflower with a Rarebit Sauce. For color, add the Holiday Apple Salad, and some Pickled Watermelon Rind. The most traditional of all the Christmas recipes we know is a Plum Pudding with Hard Sauce.

Pickled Watermelon Rind

2   Lbs. watermelon rind
2   cups vinegar
2   cups water
4   cups sugar
1   stick cinnamon
1   tsp. whole cloves
1   tsp. allspice
1   lemon, sliced thin

Select melon with thick, tender rind. Cut away the green rind, and get rid of the pink pulp. Cut what is left into squares, approximately 1" square. Dissolve ¼ cup salt in each quart of water needed to cover pieces of rind. Soak rind in this brine overnight. Wash in fresh water until tender. Combine spices and lemon and boil together for 5 minutes. Cook rind in syrup until rind is clear and tender. Pack pickles in hot sterilized jars and fill with hot syrup. Seal and label. This recipe should make about 2 pints. (Spices may be tied up in a small cheesecloth bag if you wish).

Cauliflower with Rarebit Sauce

Trim and wash a whole head of cauliflower. Season with salt and place in a colander over boiling water. Cover and steam until tender. Serve whole in a large bowl but keep it hot, or reheat it when you are ready to pour the Rarebit Sauce over it.

RAREBIT SAUCE:

Melt 1 Tbsp. butter and add ½ Lb. Cheddar cheese, cut into bits. Stir in ½ tsp. dry mustard and a dash of red pepper. Gradually add ½ cup of beer and continue to stir well. While still stirring, add 1 slightly beaten egg. Be prepared in advance to serve this immediately. It also goes well over broiled tomatoes, ham, steaks, broccoli, and other vegetables.

Roast Ducks in Orange Sauce

Ducks should be washed and dried, prior to cooking. They will taste better if you fill the cavity with an onion, an apple, a couple of stalks of celery and a few carrots before you roast them in a baking pan. Melt 2 Tbsp. of butter in the pan before you put the ducks in. Allow a roasting time of 20 minutes to the pound. Rub the ducks well with salt and pepper, and roast in a hot 400 degree oven for 15 minutes. Reduce heat to 350 degrees and continue to roast. Make the recipe for the sauce (below) and follow instructions about basting the duck as the roasting progresses. Remove vegetables when finished.

ORANGE SAUCE:

When the ducks are close to being done, remove them from the pan and pour some of the fat off from the roasted duck as it cooks. Mix 5 Tbsp. of flour and ¼ cup of cold water, and blend. Deglaze the pan with a can of heated chicken stock and scrape the bottom of the pan. Continue to blend, stir and cook, then add 1 cup of orange juice, 1 tsp. of orange zest (sliver the orange part of the skin only, not the white), and add a little lemon juice and lemon zest. While the sauce is cooking, add 2 Tbsp. of Teriyaki sauce, 1 Tbsp. of brown sugar, and 1 cup of port wine. Stir in ¼ cup chopped green onions and 2 mashed cloves of garlic. When the sauce begins to really cook down and thicken, put the ducks back in and baste continually. The duck will acquire a fine thick glaze. If fat rises to the top, remove it with a spoon. Continue to cook until the sauce becomes thickened and bubbly.

Fruited Bread Dressing

Crumble and stir fry one pound of bulk sausage (regular, mild, or hot) in a large frying pan. As it starts to brown, add ½ cup of chopped onions. When the onions are soft and sausage is browned, remove from the fire and pour into a large mixing bowl. Prepare to add 1 pkg. of stuffing mix. Read directions on the package, adding required amounts of butter or margarine and water to the bowl of sausage. Stir, add the stuffing mix and one cup of fruit (cherries, cranberries, or chopped apples, or you may want to use a combination of these fruits). Toss lightly to combine all ingredients. Pour into a buttered casserole dish. Put a few pats of butter on top and bake in a 350 degree oven for approximately 1 hour, until the top is nicely browned and crisp, but not burnt.

Potato Puffs

Mash hot cooked potatoes, and whip them well. Add 2 Tbsp. of butter, 2 eggs, beaten, and salt. Beat until all ingredients are blended. Spoon or pipe into oven-proof ramekins and pull it up to a peak in each one. Run under broiler until lightly browned.

Holiday Apple Salad

Cut 6 apples into small cubes. Peel or not , as you choose, but the red skin adds color to the salad. As you work, toss apple cubes in a little orange juice to keep fresh. Add orange sections from 4 oranges, 1 cup of soaked and drained raisins, 1 cup chopped pecans, and 1 cup miniature marshmallows. Mix mayonnaise into it. The amount depends on your taste.

Plum Pudding with Hard Sauce

½	Lb. raisins
½	Lb. currants
⅛	Lb. candied orange peel
1	oz. citron
¾	cup finely chopped suet
⅛	tsp. allspice
⅛	tsp. grated nutmeg
½	cup flour
1¼	cup bread crumbs
4	eggs
⅝	cup light brown sugar
2	tsp. cinnamon
1	tsp. ginger
½	cup currant jelly

Cut citron and orange peel fine. Mix dry ingredients. Mix liquid ingredients. Combine dry and liquid ingredients together. Fill greased molds ⅔ full and steam for 4 hours. Steam again 1 to 2 hours immediately before using. Serve hot with warmed Hard Sauce.

HARD SAUCE:

Combine ⅓ cup butter, ½ tsp. vanilla or lemon extract, 1 cup powdered sugar. Add sugar gradually to creamed butter. Whiskey or rum may be added to this.

*A*ll Southern ladies just love to set a pretty tea table and get out Granny
French porcelain dessert set with the moss rose design. Then they go to work with
vengeance, creating all sorts of Tea party Canapes, and Jam Filled Cookies, an
Marguerites. The Springerle Cookie recipe also came from immigrant ancestors, a
many of the other recipes in this book have. We end the book with this scene, showin
you the epitome of Southern hospitality.

Ginger Snaps

cup shortening
cup sugar
cup hot coffee
cup molasses
cups cake flour
tsp. salt
tsp. soda
tsp. ginger
tsp. clover
tsp. cinnamon

Cream shortening and sugar thoroughly. Add the hot coffee to the molasses and add to the creamed mixture. Sift dry ingredients together. Add gradually to liquid mixture. Chill thoroughly. Roll out on a pastry cloth to ⅛" thick, cut out, and bake in a 350 degree oven for 17 minutes.

Coconut Macaroons

¼ cups almonds
tsp. sugar
Tbsp. grated lemon peel
egg whites, beaten
cup sugar
Tbsp. lemon juice
cup grated fresh or angel
flake coconut

Grind almonds coarsely. Combine cinnamon and grated lemon peel. Beat egg whites very stiff, fold in sugar and continue beating. Fold in lemon juice with almond mixture and blend. Stir in shredded coconut. Drop from a tsp. onto ungreased heavy paper. Bake 30 minutes at 250 degrees. Remove from paper while still slightly warm.

Marguerites with Pecans

1   cup sugar
½   cup water
4   marshmallows
2   egg whites
2   Tbsp. shredded coconut
½   tsp. vanilla
1   cup chopped walnuts
    Saltine crackers

Boil sugar and water until syrup will spin a long thread when dropped from the tines of a fork. Remove from fire. Add marshmallows cut in pieces. Do not stir. Pour into stiffly beaten egg whites. Beat until stiff. Add chopped nuts and vanilla. Pile on crackers and bake in a 325 degree oven until delicately browned.

Aunt Betty Sue's Butter Cookies

These are not super sweet cookies. Cream together 2 sticks of butter and ½ cup powdered sugar. Add 1½ tsp. vanilla, 2 cups flour, and 1 cup finely chopped pecans. Chill in refrigerator for a few minutes. Roll into 1" balls. Place on a greased cookie sheet. Flatten with fork in one direction, and then turn fork at right angles, and press again to form a waffle pattern. Bake at 375 degrees for 10 to 12 minutes, or until lightly browned. Let them rest for a few minutes and remove from the sheet. These may be stored for a week in a can with a tightly fitted lid.

Jam Filled Sugar Cookies

½   cup butter
1   cup sugar
1   egg
1   Tbsp. milk
½   tsp. vanilla
½   tsp. salt
1   tsp. baking powder
1½ cups flour

Let butter soften, beat in sugar, egg, milk, and vanilla. Mix and sift dry ingredients. Mix well with the butter mixture. Add flour, if needed, to make dough fairly stiff. Roll out to ¼" thickness. Cut circles. Use a small cutter and cut out center of half the cookies. Put these on top of the others. Fill each with jam, and bake at 375 degrees about 8 minutes. Lift from baking sheet with spatula and cool. Store in tightly covered container, with wax paper between them.

Petal Sandwiches

Cut small circles out of bread with a round or scalloped cookie cutter. Spread with Pimento cheese. Separate the yolks from the whites of boiled eggs. Cut "petals" (thin strips with points) from the white part and place 6 on each circle with the points radiating out. Mash the yolks with a fork and add enough mayonnaise to hold it together. Put a small mound in the center of each circle. Chill until serving time.

Grandma Hetty's Springerle Cookies

2   eggs
1   cup sugar
     Grated rind of lemon
2   cups cake flour
½   tsp. baking powder
⅛   tsp. salt
1-2 tsp. anise seed (or use 2 drops
     of anise oil)

If the eggs are large, you may need to incorporate extra flour as you work with the dough. It must not stick to the board. Beat eggs until very well thickened. Add sugar gradually, beating until completely dissolved. Sift flour, measure, and sift again, with baking powder and salt. Add to egg and sugar mixture, mixing well as you go. If you are using anise oil, add it at this point. Roll out on floured board, to ¼" thickness. This can be cut into rounds at this point. You can put a wooden board with carved designs on it and press it down hard on the rolled out dough. Then cut the square cookies apart. These are called Springerle cookies. The anise seeds can be put in the dough for the round cookies, but if you put them in the Springerle cookies, they tend to interfere with the pattern. So — sprinkle them on the cookie sheet and then put the cookies on top of the seeds to pick them up.

Many people like to sprinkle the small colored candies on the round cookies. If you don't like anise, add lemon extract or other extracts for flavor. Let the Springerle cookies stand overnight, uncovered, to set the pattern. Bake at 350 degrees for 15 to 20 minutes until they barely turn brown.

Tea Party Canapes

Spread cream cheese on 2" squares of white or whole wheat bread. Cu squares of thinly sliced smoked salmon and place on half of the ope face sandwiches. Slice cucumbers thinly, lengthwise, and cut int squares. Place these on the other half of the bread squares and dus lightly with paprika. A dollop of mild mango chutney goes nicely on th smoked salmon.

Pecan Mini Pies

Cut circles of prepared folded pie crust, to fit individual pie pans. Pres the trimmings together and work the dough well. Roll it out again an cut more circles, if you need them.

FILLING:

Beat 3 eggs slightly. Add ½ cup sugar, ¼ tsp. salt, 1 cup light corn syrup and ½ tsp. vanilla, and mix together well. Stir in broken pieces o pecans, and mix well. Save a few large halves to garnish the center o each little pie. Press the pie dough into the individual pie pans carefully leaving enough on the edge to crimp before you bake them. Pour the fill ing into them and bake in a 300 degree oven. Fill them about half full o they will bubble over. About halfway through the baking, dip the peca halves into some butter and place one half pecan on the top of each pie I suggest dipping it into the filling before you place it. Bake until the are nicely browned on top. They will bake faster than a large pie, s watch them carefully.

ORDER FORM

If you would like to order additional copies of this book or sample some of our other fine products, please fill out the form below and mail to:

YOUR POINT OF PURCHASE RETAILER
OR
R.A.L. ENTERPRISES
Suite 136, 5000 A West Esplande Ave. · Metaire, LA 70006

TITLE	COST		QUANTITY	TOTAL
COOKIN' IN HIGH COTTON	**64 PGS.**	**$7.95**	_____	_____
Cookin' New Orleans Style	64 pgs.	$7.95	_____	_____
Cookin' Country Cajun (Hard Cover)	64 pgs.	$9.95	_____	_____
Cookin' Country Cajun (Soft Cover)	64 pgs.	$7.95	_____	_____
Cookin' on the Mississippi (Hard Cover)	64 pgs.	$9.95	_____	_____
Cookin' on the Mississippi (Soft Cover)	64 pgs.	$7.95	_____	_____
Historic Houses of the Deep South	64 pgs.	$12.95	_____	_____
Favorite Recipes from New Orleans	64 pgs.	$7.95	_____	_____
Southern Seafood Sampler	64 pgs.	$7.95	_____	_____
Favorite Drinks of New Orleans	32 pgs.	$4.95	_____	_____
Plantation Country Guide	64 pgs.	$7.95	_____	_____
New Orleans - Birthplace of Jazz	56 pgs.	$7.95	_____	_____
New Orleans - Crescent City	32 pgs.	$4.95	_____	_____
Laminated New Orleans Placemats	Set of 4	$9.95	_____	_____
Laminated Louisiana Plantation Placemats	Set of 4	$9.95	_____	_____
Laminated Mississippi Plantation Placemats	Set of 4	$9.95	_____	_____
New Orleans Coloring Book	32 pgs.	$4.95	_____	_____
Louisiana / Mississippi Coloring Book	32 pgs.	$4.95	_____	_____
Recipe Box Cards	Set of 10	$5.95	_____	_____
			Postage & Handling	$2.00
			TOTAL	_____

☐ Check Enclosed   ☐ Visa   ☐ MasterCard   ☐ American Express   ☐ Discover

Card Number _____ Expiration Date _____

Name _____

Address _____

City _____ State _____ Zip _____

Daytime Phone (___) _____

All items are satisfaction guaranteed and your purchase will be promtly refunded if returned within 30 days.
Please allow two-four weeks for delivery. No foreign orders please.